Teaching creative writing
in the primary school

D0569549

Martia
Tel: (

31
2 2

1 0

1 1

Teaching creative writing in the primary school

Delight, entice, inspire!

Julie MacLusky and Robyn Cox

 Open University Press

Open University Press
McGraw-Hill Education
McGraw-Hill House
Shoppenhangers Road
Maidenhead
Berkshire
England
SL6 2QL

email: enquiries@openup.co.uk
world wide web: www.openup.co.uk

and
Two Penn Plaza, New York, NY 10121-2289, USA

Open University Press 2011

A catalogue record of this book is available from the British Library

ISBN10: 0-33-524279-0
ISBN13: 978-0-33-524279-5
eISBN: 978-0-33-524280-1

Library of Congress Cataloging-in-Publication Data
CIP data has been applied for

Typeset by Aptara Inc., India
Printed in the UK by Bell & Bain Ltd, Glasgow

Fictitous names of companies, products, people, characters and/or data that may be
used herein (in case studies or in examples) are not intended to represent any real
individual, company, product or event.

This book is dedicated to our daughters, Bella MacLusky, Ellie Gonzalez and Olivia Gonzalez, with thanks for their patience whilst their mothers wrote this together.

Thanks also to staff at Hereford Cathedral Junior School and St Barnabas Church of England Primary School, and to Sian Dooley, Phil Davies and Vanessa Hall at Tadworth Primary School in Surrey.

Finally to Dr Jill Terry at the University of Worcester, who first suggested that Robyn Cox and I go for a coffee and talk about a book.

Contents

An introduction to creative writing

1 Models of teaching

This book sets out to provide writing workshop exercises which are used in the teaching of professional writing but which have been sculpted and focused to work in the primary classroom. Each exercise has a series of student outcomes which are aligned to those required for primary classrooms in England and specifically the outcome statements from the Primary National Strategy. This, of course, is a knotty task, particularly when curriculum in England is subject to the manoeuvrings of governments and political imperatives, sometimes prompted by economic conditions and national ambitions.

This is a wider discussion and is clearly outside the remit of this book but will be revisited as a touchstone in Chapters 3 and 9. Chapter 9 disengages with the specificity of curriculum and performance outcomes and has as its focal point the larger agenda of creativity and a discussion of both performance and production in writing.

It is a commonly held belief that before we can start thinking about both writing and the teaching of writing, we need to think about how writing has been theorized both in its composition and pedagogy since the introduction of compulsory schooling and the desire of governments for universal literacy. Thus Chapter 1 outlines theoretical approaches to the teaching of writing in the primary school. By reviewing key pedagogical theories and models of writing curriculum for primary schools it is hoped that readers of this book will be able to make informed decisions in regard to the implementation of the exercises in Chapters 4 to 8.

The skills model of teaching English

The skills approach to the teaching of writing had its roots in the subject-centred approach to English teaching which emerged at the end of the First World War when schooling became available to the masses. The subject-centred or skills approach was a combination of the recognition of the need for universal literacy and also the recognition that in a Europe facing the economic and political challenges of a very difficult peace, that the need for an understanding of Englishness represented by the 'literary canon' became important. The teaching of writing at this time was not particularly focused on the individual composing process, but rather on the copying of model texts with a focus on the presentation of this written text. Thus, much time was devoted in schools to make sure that handwriting was perfectly executed.

Skills approaches to teaching writing focus on issues of form and mechanics such as spelling, grammar and sentence structure. This is why some classes had learners copy down model essays – in order on the one hand to perfect handwriting and on the other to gain some insight into how good essays flowed and were structured. The idea was that once competence in the mechanical tools was achieved, students could attempt to compose a series of arguments which might lead to a written essay. Effective communication of ideas was the target, and some classrooms had students who never got to compose their own texts, other than notes of thank you or greetings.

At the same time as the focus on handwriting, the teaching of spelling resulted in classrooms where lists of words were drilled and copied over and over again, until long and complicated spellings became learnt. However texts were also composed that required the words which the learners could spell.

Formal teaching of grammar also took place in these classrooms, often using the learning and application of rules derived in part from the grammatical analysis practice familiar to the Latin classroom. Again all this practice might have made the student proficient in the individual skills of writing but original writing was not encouraged, nor was it the designated outcome of these skills lessons. When the composition of texts was the outcome of a lesson, it was usual that all students in the class wrote the same text in response to a title given by the teacher. An example of one of these titles might be 'My Holiday', 'An Unexpected Find' or 'An Exciting Day Out'.

The other dominant aspect of English teaching at this time was the teaching of the classics, where the passing on of a legacy of cultural knowledge to students was of paramount importance. At times this body of knowledge was made up of what has become known as the 'literary canon,' and included such authors as Dickens, Shakespeare and the Romantic Poets.

Commentators have said that this approach fitted an era where initial literacy was in prime demand and Graff (1987: 262) even argues that literacy learning was used as an instrument to inculcate 'punctuality, respect, discipline, subordination'. Cope and Kalantzis (1993: 15) agree that 'the logic of traditional curriculum was to serve up a universal "standard", with aspirations to represent fact and cultural universality.' This focus was a way of instilling in learners knowledge of their cultural heritage, and thus to develop a well-educated citizen. During these times the theory driving pedagogy was derived from behaviourism and dialogues of control.

Another form of skills-based writing emerged at this time and was known more widely as the rhetorical approach to writing. This follows the notion that in order to produce a logical argument, a writer or orator would need to follow the lines of an argument which would be prescribed and could be taught easily to students. This derives in part from the Aristotelian approach to speech making, where the novice speaker would listen to the more expert speaker and then reproduce the structure (or rhetoric) but with their own content.

A common example of the use of the rhetorical approach to writing seen in schools, even today, is the five paragraph essay. A first paragraph which foreshadows what is to come is followed by three topic sentences; this is followed by three paragraphs which fill out the arguments outlined in the first paragraph. Then a fifth paragraph summarizes the points made in the first four paragraphs. This approach is interesting in both its resilience across time and the fact that there is no doubt that certain forms of argument and composition are prototypical of how we argue and communicate.

The progressive approach to teaching English

The progressivist writings of John Dewey and Maria Montessori in the early twentieth century, gave rise to the child-centred approach to teaching

English. However changes in classroom practice and curriculum direction took some time to come about, and it was not until the post-Second World War years that Whitehead (1966: 15) writes about the perceived centrality of the individual and creativity: 'The child's development of language is, then, very closely bound up with his whole development as thinking and experiencing human being.'

Whitehead's (1966) commentary provided fertile ground for the further development of a child-centred English curriculum. It was thought that if the context was provided, the learner would 'grow' in or through language. The mid 1970s saw the release of *Language for Life* (Department of Education and Science (DES) 1975), a major report of a committee of inquiry into the teaching of English chaired by James Britton.

Britton (1972) wrote of language as being operational: 'To state the operational view at its simplest is to claim (a) that we learn by using language and (b) that we learn language by using it' (Britton 1972: 11). Speech as a preliminary act to writing became another of the central notions of self-expression. The need for classroom writing to be grounded in classroom talk accentuated the centrality of 'expressive' writing in the curriculum by classroom practitioners. This is taken up in greater detail in Chapter 3 using more recent practice, which is based on classroom research findings about the role of talk for writing.

The teacher took on a new and very different role from that traditionally expected in the skills model of teaching writing. The teacher became relegated to the sidelines of the teaching learning context, with his or her only job to facilitate the personal growth of the individual learner. Thus, the teacher was often watching from the sidelines of the classroom as individuals tackled the task of composing text from their own experience and for their own purpose. Gone was the title and topic sentence approach to the teaching of writing.

This was hailed as a new era in child centred education and even earned itself the title of 'The Growth Model of Language Education'. Central to this movement at the time was James Britton and the London Association of the Teachers of English (LATE). Britton (1970) argued that we move along a continuum when we communicate. At one end we use language as 'expressive' and at the other end as 'transactional' – to get things done. Britton argued that we need all four modes of language in order to 'express' and 'transact' and that these four modes need to be used together or to become 'whole'.

It is very clear that this practice contrasted strongly with the practices of the subject-centred paradigm that had used literacy learning as a gatekeeping process, which at times denounced the child's experience and replaced this with an immersion in 'high culture' through literature. The child-centred model of the teaching of English was part of a wider set of beliefs and practices in curriculum that focused on an 'open' or 'progressive' ideology in education. Furthermore, this was very much in keeping with the social context of the day in the 1960s and 1970s where individual freedom and self-expression was central.

The Growth Model of Language Education changed the teaching of writing forever. At the Anglo-American conference on the teaching of writing held at Dartmouth in 1966, teachers in primary school adopted a 'whole language' approach – where reading, writing, listening and speaking needed to be kept together and thus emphasized the wholeness of language. Ultimately the child-centred approach became known by various labels: the language experience approach, whole language (Goodman 1986) or the child-centred curriculum (Dixon 1975).

The process approach to teaching writing

Graves (1983) was regarded by many as the founder of the 'process writing movement,' when he reported the findings of his work with children composing in real classrooms for real purposes. This demonstrated that children could write and compose before they had perfected the skills of handwriting, grammar and spelling. Children could write and a revolution (Walshe 1981) occurred where real authentic writing workshops were initiated in classrooms. Suddenly, from the very early years on, children were encouraged to be writers and these young writers were writing.

Flower and Hayes (1977) established that writing was a messy, difficult process and that the composing process moved in fits and starts and often 'turns in on itself'. They concluded that there is a broad composing process, which includes prewriting, drafting, revising, editing and publishing. These classroom procedures became the foundation of the process writing classroom and aspects of this pedagogical practice remain in many primary classrooms, curriculum documents and primary teacher preparation programmes throughout the world.

'Process writing', as it came to be known, quickly became established as curriculum orthodoxy regardless of its effectiveness. During the 1980s teachers following these curriculum guidelines and the teaching of primary writing in schools enjoyed a golden age. This was perceived as a time when teachers set aside space, paper and pencils, typewriters, computers, dictionaries, thesauruses, editing guides and simple book-binding apparatus, supported by unlimited class time, in which children's writing practice could be encouraged.

During this golden age, the importance of the link between reading and writing and the importance of talk for writing emerged and claimed much researcher and teacher attention. In particular the importance of writing like a reader and reading like a writer motivated classroom writing lessons. A focus on author study was initiated. Bringing real writers into the primary classroom was a practice which gained attention and brought much joy to primary teachers throughout the world.

However, questions arose from these whole language classrooms. These questions formed a part of the challenge to progressivism first heard in the late 1970s, a challenge that drew upon Bernstein's early work, which states that there are two pedagogies manifest in classrooms – the visible and the invisible (Bernstein 1975). The invisible pedagogy of the child-centred approach, offers freedom for individual expression that favours middle class learners rather than students from lower socio-economic backgrounds. Thus, the invisible curriculum confirms the experiences of the middle class and English as a mother tongue student, and at the same time, disconfirm other students' experiences. Therefore, the whole language curriculum came under fire as being incapable of providing equitable experiences.

The genre approach to teaching writing

The publication of a study into language development, *Learning How to Mean* (Halliday 1975), sharply focused the debate. Halliday's study showed that language use is a series of choices which are shaped by social purposes. This seminal work by Halliday is often recognized as the genesis of the language as social construction approach. Halliday (1985) developed a functional grammar which allowed a way of looking at language use emphasizing the relationship between language in use – the text – and the context. This text/context model and the subsequent functional grammar enabled scholars and teachers to make finer observations about language use.

This approach to the teaching of writing challenges teachers to begin teaching again after being 'downgraded' to facilitators – a place they had been since the 1970s where the child-centred approach to teaching writing emerged. Christie et al. (1991: 21) argue that: 'Teaching is a deliberate act: one where teachers should intervene in, and guide, the development of their students' learning. Facilitation, like negotiation, will be one aspect of good teaching behaviour.'

When Christie et al. (1991) repositioned teaching as a deliberate act, they argued that teachers had previously been too liberal and learner centred and had become relegated to the role of observers and proofreaders in the writing classroom. They called upon the teacher to teach from a sound knowledge base to assist students in becoming improved and empowered language users.

Callaghan, Knapp and Noble (1993) introduced particular teaching learning models that they have developed on the basis of genre theory:

> In contrast to traditional grammar, with its emphasis on the rote learning of fixed rules, genre theory stresses the social context and communicative role of language. In contrast to the process learning model (where language is seen to be learnt naturally, almost by osmosis, given the right experience), genre theory emphasises the social structure that in turn structures language use.
>
> (Callaghan et al. 1993: 180)

In their research into the development of writing in the primary school, Martin and Rothery (1980) identified a number of genres from the corpus of writing being done by children in process writing classrooms. These are *observations* – about people and events; *recounts* – events sequenced over time; *narratives* – events that lead to a 'turning point' and eventually this crisis is resolved, and *serial* – problematic events, where crises and resolution occur in rapid succession.

The genre theory curriculum often recommends a teaching cycle (for example, Derewianka 1991), where the teacher models the text forms and students are encouraged to replicate these text forms using their content.

The teaching cycle typically accompanying the genre approach to writing suggested three stages: modelled writing, joint construction and independent writing. Within each of these stages of the cycle, the teacher would be able to overtly teach aspects of the text structure, grammar or even the content that the writers needed to cover. Sometimes this is seen as modelled writing, guided writing and independent writing (Hilton 2001).

Underpinning this genre-based approach to writing instruction is the use of a functional grammar of the kind proposed by Halliday (1985). This approach has enabled teachers to be very active in teaching knowledge about language and how the choices pupils make about word use can make their writing more powerful or persuasive. This was a very different focus on writing beyond the sense of writing for personal satisfaction or growth.

The teaching of creative writing?

This overview of the teaching of writing in schools and its relation to the broader field of teaching English, allows us a moment to reflect and think about our classroom practice. We are certain that primary school teachers could identify the genesis of the pedagogical practice that might be employed in writing lessons in their classrooms. This section of the chapter helps you to reflect on how you might teach writing and presents each of the teacher roles associated with the range of pedagogies in an effort to develop your confidence as a leader in the writing classroom.

A report by the Office for Standards in Education, Children's Services and Skills (Ofsted 2009), *English at the Crossroads*, shows how standards in writing compare with those in reading: 'In the primary schools visited standards in writing were considerably lower than standards in reading. Teachers, who were confident as writers themselves and could demonstrate how writing is composed, taught it effectively' (Ofsted 2009: 5).

Research conducted by Cox (2001) demonstrates that it is rare to find a primary teacher who is a writer at all, and confident writers who can demonstrate how writing is composed are even rarer. Cox's research suggests as few as one in ten teachers fall into the category of being a writer, and since her study did not specifically focus on confidence to demonstrate how writing is composed, perhaps the rate may be even lower.

Much recent work (in particular, Cremin et al. 2008) into the teaching of reading demonstrates the link between confidence, enjoyment and the ability to talk about one's reading life as a teacher. All have been shown to result in a strong causal link to the excellent teaching of reading. However, the case for writing is less well argued. In a study funded by the Department for Children, Schools and Families (DCSF), Andrews (2009) writes:

> In other words, teachers will need to be accomplished writers in themselves... They will not only be able to produce final products in this range of genres ('Here's one I made earlier...') but also to reflect on and model the processes of writing in the classroom.
>
> (Andrews 2009: 14)

This brings us to the primary purpose of this book: to support the teacher with a set of exercises which work and have operational instructions embedded in them.

However, prior to launching into these exercises let us take the time to explore the pedagogical past of the teaching of writing. Table 1.1 shows how English teaching has evolved over a hundred-year period.

Table 1.2 summarizes how the models discussed above have provided a legacy of instruction for each.

To summarize: we have a broad range of established roles operating in the writing classroom, each of which has emerged from a tradition of English teaching. Cox (2001) suggests that these roles are not exclusive and that one role should not be banished from the writing classroom as we move through time, but perhaps these four roles each have their place in the writing classroom, some in a more central role and some in a more supportive or embedded role. Teachers should be encouraged

Table 1.1 An overview of the major public theories of English education in the twentieth century

Subject centred		Progressive		Language as social construction	
Skills	Cultural heritage	Progressive	Personal growth	Critical literacy	Social functional literacy
Refinement	Cultural identity	Psychology	Sociolinguistics	Difference	Linguistics
1900	1920–1945	1935–1960	1960–1980	1985	1985

Table 1.2   The role of the teacher

Approach	Role of the student	Role of the teacher
Subject centred approach to teaching English	Students are trained	Teacher as *instructor*
Progressive approach to teaching English	Students are free to be self-directed	Teacher as *benevolent facilitator*
The process approach to writing	Student writers go through a series of stages to produce a published piece	Teacher as *manager of the writing space and facilitator of the writing purpose*
The genre approach to writing	Students are inducted into the use of language by a more skilled other	Teacher as *initiator into the language and structures of power and persuasion*

to confidently take on these roles and thus generate the ability to teach writing in a way that suits them, the learners and the curriculum.

You can be an instructor, a benevolent facilitator, a manager of the writing space and facilitator of the writing purpose, and an initiator into the language and structures of power and persuasion, because the exercises in this book will allow the teacher to take on each of the roles outlined in Table 1.2. It allows teachers to instruct, manage, initiate and facilitate, but all in the context of clearly focused exercises designed to build ideas for the content of the writing. The aim of this book is to give you wings as writing teachers and make you aware and proud of the tradition of the teacher role in the writing classroom.

Once the teacher of creative writing steps into this place, with the legacy of a hundred years of teaching writing to students, and bringing an awareness of the range of pedagogical imperatives, classroom practice and teacher roles, we are standing on the shoulders of all those excellent writing teachers that went before us. Years ago, someone had to encourage the early work of those famous writers who have been declared winners of prestigious literary awards and creators of canonical texts. With the support of these materials you can claim that space for yourself, and become a competent and confident teacher of creative writing.

Chapter 2 outlines the importance of the creative classroom and how talk is fundamental, while Chapter 3 outlines the curriculum contexts, assessment and reporting frameworks in operation.

CHAPTER 2

The classroom

Introduction

The exercises contained in Part 2 of this book are designed to enable teachers and students to model the creative process of professional writers by encouraging the use of composition and crafting techniques analogous to those employed in the working world of the creative industries. These include journalism, script development and ultimately professional authorship. However, before we can even begin to consider that the teacher of writing and her students might be able to come close to this level of engagement in the creative process we need to consider the classroom.

Classrooms by their very nature are not particularly conducive to developing creativity – it is difficult for the teacher to enable 25–30 individuals to be creative in the classroom over the course of a day. Of course there will be moments when everyone is working in pursuit of their own individual goals, but most of the time the group must be moving broadly as one towards the same outcome, albeit often with an individual product. Further exacerbating this challenge is the fact that the teacher works within system-wide constraints to do with curriculum outcomes and reporting. This was outlined in detail in Chapter 1. How, then, might a teacher enable her classroom, for some of the time, to resemble the creative world – so that real levels of creativity take place?

This chapter shows how you might develop a creative environment by providing a writing style classroom and, most importantly, developing relationships within the group which will allow these exercises to work and the students to be comfortable. This chapter covers the following areas: creativity in the world of work, creativity in the classroom, the classroom as a creative space, exploratory talk in the creative classroom, the 'dialogic classroom' and building creative relationships in the creative space; finally, there is a section about peers as writing critics, which is on how to encourage children to reflect on each other's writing that is beyond a simple 'I like this. . .' or 'things you could do better'.

Creativity in the world of work

Creative professions include writing, art, design, theatre, television, radio, motion pictures, related crafts, as well as marketing strategy, some aspects of scientific research and development, product development, some types of teaching and curriculum design, and more. By some estimates, approximately 10 million US workers are creative professionals; depending upon the depth and breadth of the definition, this estimate may be double.

The so-called 'creative industries' in the UK generate wealth through the creation and exploitation of intellectual property or through the provision of creative services. Creative industries make up the fastest growing sector of the UK economy and 7.9 per cent of the UK gross domestic product (Department for Culture, Media and Sport (DCMS) 2006). An increasing amount of the British economy is now made up of small businesses or organizations employing fewer than five people and with a turnover of less than £500,000. These small enterprises are making their mark on the landscape of the working world and are often forms of creative industries. Employment and education are inextricably linked, with the latter providing the qualified and skilled workforce that so many small industries require.

Therefore, if there are a large number of small creative industries, these industries need employees who are skilled but able to think in imaginative ways. Bob Sutton in *Business Week* (26 March 2006) states that 'the best candidates in the future will possess a creative ability that comes from working with different kinds of people on challenging projects.' How can education enable learners to meet the demands of working in this environment?

When we take time to ponder this answer we realize with an almost lightning bolt of understanding, perhaps something fundamental is being neglected here. Teaching is by its very nature a creative endeavour; when we teach we are constantly creating new contexts and generating new ways of presenting learning to children. There are others who refer to teaching as creative; in fact Loveless (2005: 20) writes: 'I believe that teaching is a creative activity that requires approaches to imagination, inspiration, engagement, improvisation and interactive relationships that the more commonly accepted creative professions demand.'

Teaching is a creative industry and the raw material that teachers labour with is children and learning. Thus education should be positioned as the stronghold of creativity.

Creativity in the classroom

So just what is creativity? The definition of creativity emerges as the pressing question when one begins to discuss creativity in the classroom. Is it just imagination, construction and being bold? Cowley (2005) identifies a list of key words which she says are commonly thought of as making up creativity: it should be imaginative, original, new, of value, and purposeful. This is a good start – creativity is all those things, but it does not really give us guidance on how to think about developing creativity in our classroom.

Wallas (1926), a contemporary of Dewey, studied the writings of creative people and came up with what some consider the classic description of the creative process. He suggests the following stages:

- *Preparation*: gathering information, thinking about the problem and coming up with ideas.
- *Incubation*: not thinking consciously about the problem but going on with normal activities.
- *Illumination*: the point where the ideas suddenly fit together and the solution becomes clear.
- *Verification*: solution checked for practicality, effectiveness and appropriateness.

Nolan (2004) goes a little further and suggests that there are three aspects to creativity: creative thinking, creative behaviour and creative action. It is worth considering this in further detail to get us thinking more about our creative classroom:

- *Creative thinking* means generating new ideas, concepts, wishes, goals, new perceptions of problems. What is generated is new thoughts which in themselves do not change anything in the real world unless they are implemented in some way (Nolan 2004: 1).
- *Creative behaviour* covers those behaviours which facilitate the creative process. The first step is to suspend judgement (Nolan 2004: 1).
- *Creative action* means actually doing new things, including doing things for the first time as well as 'doing things which are new to the world' (Nolan 2004: 1).

Our goal should be to create a classroom with space to develop these types of creative activity. The next section shows how the frameworks of both Nolan (2004) and Wallas (1926) are seamlessly embedded within the exercises in this book.

The classroom as a creative space

The idea of the classroom as a creative space is central to the following chapters. The classroom as a creative space requires a focus on the main tool for mediating the classroom, which is, of course, language. The work of Bakhtin (1981) suggested that all language, either written or spoken, carries with it evaluative undertones and those words are filled with the history of their use together with the values associated with their use. This is particularly meaningful when one thinks about classroom interaction between teachers and pupils and that these deeper meanings and undertones often mediate classroom interaction. Thus, thinking about the type of dialogue between teacher and learner is vital if we want to establish the classroom as a strong learning environment.

Wells (1999) draws our further attention to a substantial body of research conducted by researchers, often in tandem with classroom teachers, which focuses on the role of language in learning and language in the classroom. Wells (1999) favours this Bahktinian emphasis on the importance of genuine dialogue in the classroom, where the teacher has a critical role in initiating and guiding this dialogue and has the capacity to support or subdue a learner in the classroom. We need to think of the classroom not only as a place for the setting up of learning activities, but also as a place that encourages the construction of a classroom community, where all learners are equally involved in the search for understanding and the dialogue through which this is accomplished flourishes.

The legacy of the work of Vygotsky (1962, 1978) and the notion of a social learning space suggests that learning occurs mainly through linguistic interaction and dialogue, with the more learned other being central to this process. Vygotsky's conception of the 'zone of proximal development' (ZPD) allows the learner to experiment with new ideas in a safe, structured environment. Dialogue and talk can supply 'scaffolding' where teachers can initiate and guide students through the taught content. Bruner's (1978) own work builds upon Vygotsky's and suggests that one person can become very closely associated with another's learning: '[Scaffolding] refers to the steps taken to reduce the degrees of freedom in carrying out some task in that the child can concentrate on the difficult skills she is in the process of acquiring' (Bruner 1978: 19).

Clearly, the focus here is on children constructing their own view of reality and hence we can call this type of pedagogy 'constructivist'; when we acknowledge the social nature of the classroom space, the type of creative classroom learning space that we are seeking will be a social constructivist classroom one.

Exploratory talk in the creative classroom

Early investigations of classroom talk established that the most common form of classroom talk is teacher talk (Barnes 1976). Many studies over a period of time (see, for example, Sinclair and Coulthard 1992) identified what has become known as the initiation–response–evaluation or feedback (IRE or IRF) as the dominant mode of classroom talk. A very telling example of this can be seen in this example of teacher–student interaction.

> *Teacher:*　　Around what century was the English civil war fought?
> *Student A:*　The seventeenth century.
> *Teacher:*　　Yes, very good. Can you tell us what part of the seventeenth century?
> *Student A:*　During the 1640s to 1650s.
> *Teacher:*　　Excellent.

Clearly this is a very acceptable way of teaching; however, the teaching and learning relationship requires many more variations of classroom interaction to be taking place as well. In the example above there is only one student speaking; the teacher strongly controls who speaks, and is the only one who is allowed to speak without asking permission or being invited (Mercer and Dawes 2008).

Further work by Mercer et al. (1999), which became known as 'exploratory classroom talk', can give us some direction here. Broadly, exploratory talk is that 'in which partners engage critically but constructively with each other's ideas. Statements and suggestions are sought and offered for joint consideration. These may be challenged and counter-challenged, but challenges are justified and alternative hypotheses are offered' (Mercer et al. 1999: 97).

Mercer et al. (1999) set out to explore whether or not a classroom where talk and dialogue was central was capable of increasing children's use of language for reasoning and collaborative activity. Their study found that:

(a) using 'exploratory talk' helps children to work more effectively on problem-solving tasks;
(b) using a specially designed programme of teacher-led and group-based activities, teachers can increase the amount of 'exploratory talk' used by children working together in the classroom;
(c) children who have been taught to use more 'exploratory talk' make great gains in individual scores on a test of reasoning than do children who have not had such teaching.

(Mercer et al. 1999: 108)

So what is exploratory talk? How might we harness its obvious potential in the creative classroom, as we want children who can use problem solving and reasoning to parallel this notion of creative spaces in creative industries? The following set of conditions can assist us in developing a creative space in the primary classroom:

1. Participants must have a good shared understanding of the point and purpose of the activity.
2. The 'ground rules' for the activity should encourage a free exchange of relevant ideas and the active participation of all involved.

3. Partners must have to talk to do the task, so their conversation is not merely an incidental accompaniment
4. The activity should be designed to encourage co-operation, not competition, between partners.

(Mercer 1995: 98)

Most pedagogical models and curriculum structures are primarily focused on individual achievement rather than group processes, so that setting up classrooms which enable teachers to provide learning and interaction of the type discussed above may involve changing from a more formal placement of desks and furniture. This will be further discussed at the end of this chapter.

The 'dialogic classroom'

To this point we have placed talk at the centre of the creative classroom, and found that by referring to the importance attached by Bakhtin (1981) to the words used in the teaching learning environment and Wells' strong suggestion that only genuine dialogue should be used, and that there should be limits on the use of IRF. Finally, Mercer's research has established that problem-solving and reasoning scores increase when learners take part in genuine, interactive and thoughtful talk. We then come to Robin Alexander's (2001) research, which owes its origins to his comprehensive international comparative study, which demonstrates that there is much greater emphasis on informal teacher talk in Britain and the United States than in India, France or Russia. Through comparative analysis of classroom interactions in five countries (United States, England, France, India and Russia) he identified five categories of classroom talk that he observed in use:

Rote: drilling of facts, ideas and routines;
Recitation: the accumulation of knowledge and understanding through questions which might have clues embedded in the question itself;
Instruction/exposition: telling the pupils what to do, imparting information or facts, principles or procedures;

> *Discussion:* the exchange of ideas with a view to sharing information and solving problems;
>
> *Dialogue:* achieving common understanding through structured, cumulative questioning and discussion which guide and prompt, reduce choices, minimise risk and error.
>
> (Wolfe and Alexander 2008: 3)

Wolfe and Alexander (2008: 3) suggest that a 'radical shift in thinking is not what is required but a movement towards change by increasing awareness of possibilities.' From those identified through the research above Alexander identifies the two final different forms of talk – discussion and dialogue, which have the strongest potential for cognitive development.

What is meant by dialogic interactions? A good definition is that supplied by Wolfe and Alexander (2008: 4): 'In dialogic interactions, children are exposed to alternative perspectives and required to engage with another person's point of view in ways that challenge and deepen their own conceptual understandings.'

The importance of Alexander's work has been in the emphasis he places upon the difference between 'interactive' teaching as understood by teachers, and the more focused idea of 'logic and rational argument' (Alexander 2008: 4). Interactive teaching has existed in primary classrooms in England for many years but both Mercer's 'exploratory talk' and Alexander's 'dialogic teaching' are well-articulated calls for teachers to focus much more on bringing children to greater cognitive understanding by means of very well-designed classroom tasks.

Building creative relationships in the creative space

The previous section has clearly shown by the discussion of research and theorizing that primary classrooms are fertile places for talk, interaction, dialogue and creativity. This, together with the points made in Chapter 1 about the range and fusion of teacher roles that the teacher can assume when teaching writing, places you as the teacher in a confident position to move forward into the exercises.

Nevertheless, there is another group in the classroom that we have not talked about yet and that is the pupils. What is their role in the creative classroom? Can they help build this creative space or is it just another curriculum essential for the teacher to activate? We are not sure – a key here is the establishment of a creative classroom space where genuine and trusting relationships between the teacher and the learners and between learners can be established.

Early work in researching creativity emphasized the creative individual working alone and that creativity has been thought of as an individual attribute (Torrance 1987). More recent work talks about creativity as emerging from a system and an investment (Sternberg and Lubart 1995). However, it is not until we come to Sawyer's (2004) work that we find out about research which suggests that conversation situated in a discipline is necessary for the development of creativity in the classroom. Sawyer (2004) talks of 'discipline improvisation' to emphasize the balance of structure and freedom and thus the collaborative nature of enquiry in the classroom community and the role of peer co-participation.

Sawyer's work gives us a 'blueprint' for our creative space, creative relationships and the creative writing exercises in Part 2 of this book. He suggests: 'In disciplined improvisation, teachers locally improvise within the planned curriculum structure and knowledge goals' (Sawyer 2004: 16). What might be distinct about this? Teachers have always been improvising due to local contextual issues, resources and/or specific learner needs – it is the heart of our work. But Sawyer (2004) offers more by recognizing the teacher as a creative professional rather than as a technician delivering a predetermined curriculum. This requires teachers to have knowledge of the curriculum, an understanding of the required learner outcomes and the capacity to facilitate group improvisation effectively.

Wragg (2005), in an interview about the place of creativity in the classroom, suggests: 'To have a really creative climate what you need is first of all freedom from fear, because fear is not a good motivator for creativity' and he goes on to reiterate 'Creativity embodies risk' (Wragg 2005: 186, 188). Where does this put teachers and pupils? In my view it puts them exactly at the heart of where this chapter started, with the idea that together pupils and teachers can build this creative space.

Seeing creativity as emerging from dialogue is presented by Craft (1997) when she suggests that the notion of 'being in relationship' was seen as a dynamic interaction between teacher and learner, learner and learner, and also between the learner and the discipline itself. For example, to be good storytellers, children need to learn that they do not have to itemize every single event that happens. In young writers the story can too easily get lost in the overwhelming amount of detail that is used. Yet readers love to have their imaginations engaged so that they are forced to fill in the gaps.

There are many other examples of economical storytelling:

- Peter Pan was once a 'real boy' himself, yet we work this out through clues planted in the text.
- In *The Three Little Pigs* we do not have the whole story about why the pigs must leave home, or what their lives were like before they left.
- In *The Lion, the Witch and the Wardrobe* we do not know why the children are taken to Narnia in the first place, or exactly what happens during the thousand or more years that they are away from Narnia before they return in the book *Prince Caspian*.

A beginning writer might be afraid that 'creative writing' entails sitting in front of a blank computer screen or piece of paper, and somehow dreaming up a story about dragons, monsters, pirates, romance, all from nowhere. They may feel that 'real' writers have been given a gift from somewhere 'up on high', and simply wait to channel this power through their fingertips and onto the page.

Professional writers look on their writing as work, and have, often over years of practice, developed the ability to find stories in their own lives and the lives of those around them. These exercises empower pupils to begin to develop a writer's ability to select elements and truths from their own lives to embellish and underpin their creative work. For a writer, no moment of living is wasted; the awful family fighting in the railway carriage becomes a useful scene in their next novel or script. The revolting uncle becomes the baddie in their next story. Through these exercises pupils can begin to understand that their own daily lives, and especially times of conflict and even pain, have incredible imaginative value.

The teacher needs to be a creative improviser and to lead pupils to learn the art of alchemy, which is the writer's talent to transform the everyday, sometimes painful or mundane into something emotionally gripping and affective. Remember Wragg's (2005: 188) words: 'Creativity embodies risk'.

Peers as writing critics

Teaching creative writing puts the emphasis on the teacher as driving the creative classroom and this presents the teacher with a series of wonderful opportunities to mix up pupils within groups and to encourage emotional sharing and the growth of empathy. The sharing of personal stories helps develop bonds across diverse groups. Children will find out that the most painful events of their lives are shared events, and those feelings of loss, bereavement and grief generate similar reactions and emotions in all of us. It can result in a breakthrough in communication between tougher and weaker kids, between bullies and the bullied, between children who would normally be oppositional in character and temperament, because it is harder to objectify and disregard the feelings of someone you have shared an emotional truth with.

Group and pair work enables pupils to share family stories and, as pupils are encouraged to make suggestions as to how each other's stories should end, and in situations where pupils are using material that is auto-biographical, they are in fact making suggestions as to how another pupil can resolve conflict within their own life. Thus the exercises can build empathy and improve the ability of the children to empathize with the problems of others within their class. As class members listen to their stories, they will want to work out ways to make the story better – things they would like to know more about – something that might make the story more exciting.

To maintain the feeling of safety, teachers need to restate regularly that all the stories talked about in class are fiction. This means that even if you base a story upon something that really happened to you, by the time you have written it down, perhaps changed the colour of a character's hair, added a thunderstorm, a monster or two, you have transformed it into fiction. Establishing these parameters will help children to tell stories that they might otherwise consider too scary, risky or emotional to share.

Conclusion

Rolls-Royce sends its engineering trainees to spend a week at Tate Liverpool? Why would they do that? The company want to create 'a new model for learning' which integrated the 'acquisition of technical skills with the development of personal, critical and creative thinking skills through engagement with the work of artists' (Arts and Business, MMC Arts, Business and Employees Award, 2004).

Creativity here can be the coach and horses that ignites the enthusiasm and drags progress in all other areas forward. Some pupils might struggle in a lesson of pure grammar, being taught how to use speech marks and parts of speech, but when this lesson has immediate, satisfying and practical application, in enabling them to make their characters talk, then they can see, and thus grasp the point. In Chapter 3 we find out about how the Primary National Strategy and the requirement for statutory assessment can further structure the context for the exercises that follow.

3 The curriculum

The National Curriculum context

In Britain, the government has always had an ambitious agenda to improve schools, accelerate pupils' learning and close the achievement gap between rich and poor students. The school systems in Britain have strong results with a rising profile for example at Key Stages 1, 2 and 3; the results are the best that they have ever been across the broad range of groups. Clearly, the government has been aware of the success of its educational reforms at the micro-level through Standardized Achievement Test (SAT) results, Ofsted inspection results and other measurable achievements.

The National Curriculum (ages 5 to 16) was introduced in 1988 under the Education Reform Act. The National Curriculum consists of the following programmes of study in the primary school: Key Stage 1 (5–7-year-old children) and Key Stage 2 (7–11-year-old children). Following the introduction of the National Curriculum, Key Stage 1 statutory tests were introduced in 1991 with Key Stage 2 being introduced in 1995. We are now operating in a context where more than 20 years of curriculum and testing has produced a school system that is operating at a highly functioning level.

In May 2010 the incoming coalition of Conservative and Liberal Democrats may lead to a refocusing of curriculum and assessment across primary education in England. The previous Labour government had accepted recommendations put forward by Sir Jim Rose to implement a new primary curriculum from September 2011. However, while there is certainty that the recommendations of the Rose Review (DCSF 2009) may provide some foundations for the future primary curriculum, strong differences in educational viewpoints suggest that while statutory testing will remain, curriculum guidelines and directions may change.

For example a statement on the National Curriculum website suggests:

> Ministers are committed to giving schools more freedom from unnecessary prescription and bureaucracy. They have always made clear their intentions to make changes to the National Curriculum that will ensure a relentless focus on the basics and give teachers more flexibility than the proposed new primary curriculum offered.
> (www.education.gov.uk/schools/teachingandlearning/ curriculum/a0061705/changes-to-the-national-curriculum, accessed 10 November 2010)

The main indicators for how the National Curriculum is implemented in relation to writing come to us through the Primary National Strategy and it is this framework which will now be discussed.

Statutory content of the National Curriculum in writing

In England the National Curriculum (Department for Education and Employment (DfEE) 1999) provides a close evaluation of the elements that make up writing instruction, presented below in an adapted form. The main area of the National Curriculum related to writing is EN3 (Writing), which provides teachers and schools with the minimum national entitlement for pupils in schools.

EN3 Writing Key Stage 1

During Key Stage 1 learners start to enjoy writing and see the value of it in learning to communicate meaning in narrative and nonfiction texts and spell and punctuate correctly. The programme of study for English and the National Literacy Strategy *Framework for Teaching* are closely related. The *Framework* provides a detailed basis for implementing the statutory requirements of the programmes of study for reading and writing. It identifies the knowledge skills and understandings under six headings: composition, planning and drafting; Standard English; language structure; punctuation; spelling; and handwriting. Discussion of the detail involved in the first category – composition, planning and drafting enables us to focus on what it is that learners need to be taught.

There are clear requirements for putting ideas in sentences using wide-ranging and adventurous vocabulary. Further to this students are expected to be able to use reading texts as models for their own writing, which will in turn provide a clear structure to organize their writing, demonstrating that they can sequence and recount events. At Key Stage 1 students are expected to understand the needs of the reader of their texts and vary their writing to suit their own writing purpose.

In terms of the breadth of study across Key Stage 1, learners should be able to engage in a range of purposes for writing, such as to communicate to others; to create imaginary worlds; to explore experience; and to organize and explain information. In terms of the form or generic forms on writing, learners at Key Stage 1 should be writing narratives, poems, notes, lists, captions, records, messages and instructions.

EN3 Writing Key Stage 2

Once learners move on to Key Stage 2 they begin to develop the understanding that writing is both essential to thinking and learning, and enjoyable in its own right. Learners use the planning, drafting and editing process to improve their work and to sustain their fiction and nonfiction writing.

In the National Literacy Strategy *Framework for Teaching*, the area of composition, planning and drafting clearly provides fertile ground for the teacher to engage in the genuine and focused teaching of writing. Learners should be taught to choose form and content to suit their purpose and at the same time think about the language and style that will best suit the reader and the textual form. Furthermore, they are encouraged to adapt and be inventive in terms of the textual form and the use of textual layout and presentation.

At this point it becomes important for learners to take advantage of skills in planning, drafting, revising and improving their drafts. Skills of proofreading and presentation are also foregrounded in lessons. Finally, at this point learners should be able to discuss their work with others in a community of learners.

Writing tasks and lessons should guarantee that learners have a broad experience in writing tasks and thus the opportunity to imagine and explore feelings and ideas, focusing on creative uses of language. Moreover, pupils should engage with ways to interest the reader, and more importantly in relation to the learning community as discussed above, to review and comment on what has been read, seen or heard, focusing on both the topic and the writer's view of it.

In terms of the form or generic forms of writing, learners at Key Stage 2 should be writing narratives, poems, playscripts, reports, explanations, opinions, instructions, reviews and commentaries.

The importance of the teacher and his or her confidence, knowledge and ability to provide lessons where learners can gain knowledge of these varied aspects of writing is vital to the implementation of Key Stages 1 and 2 EN3 aspect of the National Curriculum (DfEE 1999). There are four dominant roles described in the literature about the teaching of writing. These are: teacher as instructor, benevolent facilitator, manager of the writing space and facilitator of the writing purpose, and initiator into the language and structures of power and persuasion. The National Curriculum appears to give greatest currency to the role of the teacher as instructor with some moments where they might be a facilitator of the writing process and initiator into the language of power as well as persuasion. However, once we begin to place the layer of assessment, reporting and regulation on top of the teaching context there is a shift to the one-dimensional teacher as instructor. Can creativity flourish in this context?

Statutory assessment

Teacher assessment, statutory tests and tasks are used by schools to administer a periodic *summative* or snapshot assessment of their pupils. These results indicate whether children have made progress over a longer period and these results are thus reported to government and to parents and children.

Where assessment contributes to planning and allows teachers to determine class targets and individual targets for children, it is called *formative* assessment.

Summative statutory assessment measures progress in English against a range of published criteria. In England the criteria for Key Stages 1 and 2 are related to one of the four statements of attainment for English; however, our focus is again Attainment Target 3: Writing. Attainment targets sets out national standards of performance in English at five levels. These levels show what children should know, understand and be able to do.

Below are listed the criteria relevant to creative writing in the primary school from the National Curriculum (DfEE 1999).

Attainment Target 3: Writing (focus on composition, planning)

Level 1	Pupils' writing communicates meaning through simple words and phrases.
Level 2	Pupils' writing communicates meaning in both narrative and non-narrative forms, using appropriate and interesting vocabulary, and showing some awareness of the reader.
Level 3	Pupils' writing is often organized, imaginative and clear. The main features of different forms of writing are used appropriately, beginning to be adapted to different readers. Sequences of sentences extend ideas logically and words are chosen for variety and interest.
Level 4	Pupils' writing in a range of forms is lively and thoughtful. Ideas are often sustained and developed in interesting ways and organized appropriately for the purpose of the reader. Vocabulary choices are often adventurous and words are used for effect. Pupils are beginning to use grammatically complex sentences, extending meaning.
Level 5	Pupils' writing is varied and interesting, conveying meaning clearly in a range of forms for different readers, using a more formal style where appropriate. Vocabulary choices are imaginative and words are used precisely. Simple and complex sentences are organized into paragraphs.

(http://curriculum.qcda.gov.uk/uploads/English%201999%20programme%20of%20study_tcm8-12054.pdf, accessed 10 November 2010)

These national criteria allow children, parents and teachers to judge performance and measure the progress of children of similar ages across the primary phase.

What is good writing?

The big question which is never asked in curriculum documents, policy statements or political speeches when talking about writing is

'What is good writing?' or 'How do we know that this is a good piece of writing?' All of the rhetoric surrounding the teaching of writing – the levelling of children's texts, the political despair that national scores in reading have improved to the levels set by the previous Labour government while those in writing have been resistant to improvement – has failed to engage with this most fundamental question. Various programmes have been initiated nationally in the UK to hoist those results, for example, to bridge the gender differences and the even slower improvement by boy writers. Yet amidst this hubris of noisy policy making and relentless inspection regimes, no one seems to be asking the question, 'What is good writing?'

This chapter, with its focus on the National Curriculum, suggests that good writing must be 'the sum of the parts': all the descriptors and comments about word choice, sentence structure, paragraphing suggest that somewhere in there is buried the 'gold nugget' which is 'good writing'. We would suggest that this is not so. One writer about the teaching of writing simply says:

> What is Good Writing? You know it when you see it. It isn't that hard to tell whether a piece of writing is good or bad. You just have to read it. But things get more challenging if you have to explain why. Even harder than that is analyzing the good things a writer is doing so you can learn to use his or her techniques in your own work.
>
> (Peha 2002: 3)

However, telling us that we will know good writing when we see it is as ungainly as telling us that it is 'the sum of parts'.

MacLusky (2009) gives us something more concrete:

> Good writing must move us, emotionally. Writers, at their best, can be like puppet-masters, who know exactly how to make their characters display emotion, and how to generate an emotional response from a reader.
>
> (MacLusky 2009: 6)

This question leads us forward into Part 2 of this book, which contains exercises to develop creative writing, and further investigation into 'good writing' will take place in Part 3 of this book.

Developing creative writing

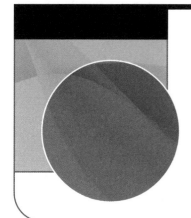

Introduction to Part 2

The exercises in Part 2 have been devised to enable pupils to grasp the essential building blocks of good writing. Each exercise is designed to build upon knowledge gained in the previous exercise, in a similar way to the most basic finger exercises followed in piano lessons. Additionally, the exercises work as 'stand alone' activities and teachers can use their knowledge of the skill level in their own classes to select individual exercises to work with.

These exercises work because they have sufficient built-in structure that pupils never have to face a blank page. Children are never told to 'just write a story', nor are they given so much structure that their stories become less skilled versions of the ones we know too well already – a princess, a castle, a knight: you fill in the gaps. Pupils completing such exercises are all too aware of how their own efforts fail to measure up and can easily become disillusioned.

A useful analogy to the way that these exercises are structured can be found in the way that horse riding is learned. You could take a group of children who wanted to learn how to ride into a lecture theatre, and deliver a wonderfully crafted ten-week course, complete with interactive tasks, pair and group work, charts to fill in and take home tests. Each child might even score 100 per cent on any assessment of this work. But if you were then to take these children and put them straight onto horses, even the most courageous might be terrified, or fall off.

The approach to creative writing in the following exercises is based upon this truth – it is only through experiencing the exercises that the learning outcomes can be achieved. The most disaffected pupils can become completely engaged when writing a story that they have ownership of, and which is subsequently acknowledged and praised by peers, during feedback sessions.

For example, a boy with a hatred of reading who, for whatever reasons, has spent too many hours watching TV, will be empowered and discover that he is able to make a significant contribution to preparatory class discussion of these exercises. He will find that the stories he knows and loves are referenced frequently in these exercises, and he will be able to access his sophisticated understanding of narrative to craft his own. It may be energizing, for the first time, to have his interests acknowledged and thus this type of pupil can become empowered through working with these exercises. We have seen this happen during our own classes, over and over again, and have every confidence that you will see a similar transformation with your own pupils.

During classroom discussion it will, however, become apparent that pupils already have very clear ideas as to what their favourite stories are, and from this, they will be able to work out those elements that should be present in the best stories, and in their own. Children in primary schools have been exposed to a great range of texts, and are already well aware of what makes a good story.

Theses exercises cannot promise to make every pupil an excellent writer but they will help any pupil to make the most of the ideas that they have and then craft them into the most compelling writing possible.

Overview of the writing chapters

Chapters 4 and 5 allow pupils to grasp the basic toolkit of essential writing skills. Through lessons based on these exercises, you will be able to see your pupils' writing develop on an incremental scale.

Chapters 6, 7 and 8 reinforce the basic toolkit of writing skills by asking pupils to develop templates for more complex stories. In this later work your pupils will be able to demonstrate their mastery of tools developed in the earlier chapters, and their attempts will be met with greater success if they have completed some of the earlier exercises.

However, it is possible to treat each exercise as a 'stand alone' activity and dip into the book at any point for a writing class that will engage pupils and generate strong writing. Ideally pupils would have experience of the key skill-building exercises in Chapters 4 and 5 before progressing to the more advanced work in Chapters 6, 7 and 8, but this is not essential. You may like to adapt the programme presented in these exercises to suit the individual needs of a specific group of pupils.

The one exception to the emphasis on completing the earlier exercises is the *Character profiles* exercise, in Chapter 8. Your pupils can be introduced to these archetypal characters at any point in their writing course and the experience will deepen and extend any writing they attempt.

Greater detail of the contents of each chapter is provided below.

Chapter 4 Character is story

4.1   Building atmosphere

Building atmosphere focuses on the potential offered by the use of the environment in storytelling, the importance of character, the beginnings of 'planting and pay-off', together with story structure.

4.2   Sharing a room

Sharing a room builds upon the potential offered by the use of the environment in storytelling, which was begun in 4.1 *Building atmosphere*. It also helps pupils further develop a concept of how characters and their possessions and interests may change over time, and how conflict can impact an environment. This exercise again stresses the central importance of character, the beginnings of 'planting and pay-off', together with story structure.

4.3   Getting ready for a date

Getting ready for a date builds upon the potential offered by the use of time-lapses in storytelling. It also helps pupils further develop a concept of how characters and their possessions and interests may change over time (introduced in 4.1 *Building atmosphere* and 4.2 *Sharing a room*) and how conflict can impact an environment. This exercise again stresses the central importance of character, the beginnings of 'planting and pay-off', together with story structure.

4.4 The character in the environment

The character in the environment further develops the power of time-lapses in storytelling first encountered in 4.3 *Getting ready for a date*. It also helps pupils further develop a concept of how the passage of time can impact both an environment and the characters who exist in it. This exercise again stresses the central importance of character, the beginnings of 'planting and pay-off', together with story structure.

4.5 Giving feedback

This section on giving feedback has important information about how to encourage your pupils to give constructive feedback about each other's work. This section needs to be read carefully as it is the key to running a successful creative writing class. Feedback builds upon the potential offered for the development and encouragement of children's writing through peer review. It is designed to deliver a wide range of social and literary skills.

Chapter 5 Story building

5.1 The object and the obstacle

The object and the obstacle focuses on the development of a strongly dramatic scene between two characters. It also reinforces elements of storytelling covered in Chapter 4 including the importance of character, the use of 'planting and pay-off', together with story structure. It introduces pupils to the concept that the frustration of the hero's desires is a fundamental component of all good storytelling.

5.2 Persuasion: unexpected arrival

Persuasion: unexpected arrival introduces pupils to the development of a strongly dramatic scene based upon conflict between two main characters.

It helps pupils understand that the drama of a story can be developed around one pivotal moment and that dialogue has multiple functions within a story.

5.3 The awkward situation

The awkward situation focuses on the development of a story in which the drama depends on either the refusal of one character to cooperate with the main character's plans, or where the environment itself is the obstacle. Seduction and persuasion are elemental scenes in storytelling and mastery of their structure will ensure that stories are compelling. This writing tool is described as engaging the reader's 'hope versus fear'. If this is secured, readers will be hooked. In addition it introduces pupils to the concept that the drama and tension in a story depends upon the obstacles that block the plans of the main character.

5.4 Making a bad situation worse

Making a bad situation worse enables pupils to begin to develop the ability to use cleverly constructed, layered conflict to add drama to their writing. Pupils may begin to develop an element of conflict resolution from this exercise, and an understanding that their own experiences of difficulties can be used as inspiration for storytelling. Pupils can also begin to understand that confession and meetings that go wrong are elemental scenes in storytelling and mastery of their structure will ensure that stories are compelling.

Chapter 6 Planting and pay-off

This chapter presents three story templates that underpin many favourite children's stories: 6.1 *The love story*, 6.2 *The misunderstanding* and 6.3 *The caper*.

This work with templates will build confidence, particularly among children who do not yet have a love of reading, but perhaps who have spent many hours watching television and films. Their familiarity with a range of genres and plots will empower such children – who might feel disenfranchised when more literary texts are discussed – to make a significant contribution to class work.

The templates are designed to generate outlines that can be used to create completed, longer fiction. Creating an outline also provides pupils with a solid understanding of the way such templates work. This will reinforce the theory that underpins the approach to writing embedded within this book: that writing is a craft that can be developed through practical exercises.

Chapter 7 Twists and turns

This chapter opens with three further story templates, 7.1 *Revolt, revenge, escape,* that once again underpin many of your pupils' favourite stories. These templates are followed by exercises that are intended as a starting point for all the more advanced exercises, from Chapter 7 onwards. These exercises are 7.2 *The world of the story,* 7.3 *Story questions* and 7.4 *Freytag's Triangle* (or the classical three-act structure).

While not designed to generate a story on their own, the questions in this chapter can be used to develop and enrich any ideas that pupils come up with for writing of their own, independent of the scenarios in this book. These questions also help prepare pupils writing earlier exercises and should be saved, as answering the questions during the drafting stage will help pupils in all future creative and non-fiction writing.

Children will be able to take their understanding of the way these fundamental templates work to help with the development of their own fiction, and to assist with their understanding as they become more sophisticated readers and viewers of texts. Some resources for following many more alternative paths to creativity are included in this section.

Chapter 8 The satisfying ending

This chapter opens with an exercise, 8.1 *Character profiles,* which is designed to help pupils create a list of archetypal characters that can be used throughout their writing. Stories where characters are either extremely good or bad, stripped of nuances and subtleties, are simplistic and sometimes boring particularly for older and more sophisticated readers. These profiles enable pupils to develop empathy for their characters, even the bad ones. By creating evil characters that are complex, good characters with major, human flaws to overcome before they can defeat evil, pupils will engage readers and create a compelling narrative.

The *Character profiles* exercise is followed by three more story templates to complete the series begun in earlier chapters: 8.2 *The supernatural*, 8.3 *The threat to world views* and 8.4 *Journey with destination*.

A final exercise, 8.5 *The escape*, enables pupils to transfer skills developed through completing the templates in this book into multiple writing formats.

The templates are designed to generate outlines that can be used to create sustained, longer fiction. Creating an outline also provides pupils with a solid understanding of the way such templates work. Children will be able to bring their understanding of the way these fundamental templates work to help with the development of any writing they do in the future.

Skills embedded in these exercises

There are lots of helpful and transferable skills that can be developed by working through these exercises, for example:

- *Characterization:* how to create compelling, original characters.
- *Plotting:* how to structure a compelling narrative that engages readers' hopes for what might happen and their fears for what might otherwise be the result.
- *Three-act structure:* how to embed the game of drama to hook readers and keep them reading.
- *Planting and pay-off:* how to plant objects, ideas, images into their stories that can be used later (paid-off) to enrich, add layers to the story and develop the plot with economy.
- *The escalation of conflict:* how to make the obstacles that their characters face truly engaging and believable.
- *The satisfying ending:* how to wrap things up and not abandon readers to 'make up their own minds' for want of an ability to work out how to reach a strong conclusion.

- *Functions of speech:* how to craft characters who speak in voices truthful to themselves; how to distinguish better between the differing functions of parts of speech and their appropriate usage. Creating dialogue that works to perform multiple functions within a narrative.

Through the preparatory exercises in Chapters 4 and 5 children can begin to unpick the major plot points of their own favourite stories, and thus begin taking ownership of the material. They will begin to understand that all great stories are intricately structured and plotted, and that their favourite authors use a palette of techniques that the children themselves can adopt, not only for this particular exercise, but also in all kinds of writing.

These exercises may build upon and develop writing techniques that are being introduced in other areas of the curriculum. For example, the fact that pupils can see that the correct use of dialogue and description is essential in a good story will provide a strong incentive to employ techniques taught elsewhere. Pupils can better grasp the need for a polished writing style when they are rewarded with positive feedback from peers about their own creative work.

Conclusion

Children will be able to take their understanding of the way these fundamental templates work to help with the development of their own fiction, and to assist with their understanding, as they become more sophisticated readers and viewers of texts.

As a consequence of the growth in the number of university-level creative writing courses, academics are starting to debate the nature of the origins of creative inspiration. In 'A Creative Writing Manifesto' commissioned for Siobhán Holland's (2003) *Creative Writing: A Good Practice Guide* (produced by the English Subject Centre), Michelene Wandor (2000: 13) suggests that the primary purpose of a creative writing course is 'to develop a combined critical and writerly understanding of ... the imaginative possibilities of language.' The theory that underpins the exercises in this book supports this, in that it is based upon a belief that it is possible to teach pupils a range of techniques that are transferable to multiple writing formats, that will enhance writing skills across the curriculum, and will, in many instances, ignite a passion for learning that would otherwise remain dormant.

Professional writers describe writing as re-writing. This means that the final version of a story may be the result of many, many drafts and re-writes, and may be nothing at all like the first draft or rough idea for that story.

The transition from being an average to a very good writer can start when an author learns that they are going to have to revise and polish an idea, a concept or a plot until it works on many levels. A good writer must be able to take into consideration the input of editors, teachers, fellow pupils and anyone else kind enough to offer some feedback, even if ultimately the advice is rejected. Through making changes at the outline stage, pupils are beginning to utilize the imaginations and ideas of others.

Pupils should be made aware that they are being offered a toolkit of classical story techniques. They can adapt these for their own use; they will find some exercises really excite them and some they will find dull. Sometimes it is difficult to write the first line, but these exercises are designed to remove the fear of a blank page for writers, and to encourage them to commence the work of writing a story with sufficient preparatory and background work that the story can flow directly from the preparatory work.

The templates within this book have been used at major film schools and in university creative writing degree programmes to successfully help generations of writers achieve their dreams, and to create compelling stories.

We hope that you, and your pupils, will find these exercises transformative, enriching and above all enjoyable. Our aim is that your pupils will mirror the assessment of one of our students who, having reluctantly been forced to take the class, wrote:

'I used to hate writing but I love it now! This is the best class I have ever taken, and the hardest work that I have ever done.'

CHAPTER

4

Character is story

4.1 Building atmosphere

Introduction

Building atmosphere focuses on the potential offered by the use of the environment in storytelling, the importance of character, the beginnings of 'planting and pay-off', together with story structure.

Building atmosphere introduces pupils to the following concepts:

- The best stories are based upon strong characters.
- Characters can be introduced through the ways that they interact with a given environment and the objects they find there.
- Characters can be developed through their actions and activities.
- An object can be used to deliver narrative, if it is planted in one scene, and then seen again later in a different way.
- An object can have its meaning and significance changed simply by changing its appearance in a different or later scene.
- A basic understanding of the conventions of genre, such as comedy, mystery and romance.
- The ways that the environment and atmosphere in which a story takes place can add drama to events.
- The ways that the environment and atmosphere of a story can be used to tell that story.

Exercise 4.1: Building atmosphere

Describe a person entering the same room three times:

1 The first time we, the readers, will know that this is going to be a scary story.
2 The second time we will know that this is going to be a very silly, funny story.
3 The third time we will know that it is going to be a story with a strong hero or heroine who will eventually, after many adventures, triumph over terrible opponents.

Each time you describe the scene, you must imagine that it is the same person who is entering the room. The room will have the same furniture and objects in it and through the window we can see the same things outside. But each time you describe the scene you are setting up a very different story. The trick is that your reader should know, just from reading the very first scene, exactly what type of story this is going to be.

Step 1: Classroom discussion – scary story

The following questions about objects that can be used in these scenes, can be used to stimulate pupil discussion for *Building atmosphere*. For example, try to think of how something simple, like a lampshade, might look, if you were telling a scary story:

- The light might sizzle on and off as the electricity supply wavers.
- There might be large spiders or slugs crawling all over it.
- The shade might be torn or covered in cobwebs.
- What are your favourite kinds of scary stories?
- What kind of scary story is it going to be?
- Do you know what kind of things you might have in a story with vampires, or werewolves, or ghosts?

Imagine if you choose to have a teddy bear, doll or toy on the bed in the room?

- If this was a scary story, then the teddy might have its stuffing strewn all over the bed. Maybe a spider crawling out of the hole where the teddy's eye used to be?

It is useful here to reference popular culture, for example stories pupils might have read in class, movies, games and TV shows.

Step 2: Classroom discussion – funny story

Ask your pupils to think of how the same lightshade might look if they were writing a funny story.

- The light might be bright.
- The shade might have a silly picture on it or a message someone has written to trick your main character.
- Maybe it would be a musical lamp, or have cartoon characters on it?
- What are your favourite kinds of funny stories, films, TV shows or poems?
- What kind of things do you have in these kinds of stories?

Imagine if you choose to have a teddy bear, doll or toy on the bed in the room?

- The teddy might be super-sized, with a red and white spotted bow round his neck and a cord that the character pulls, and the teddy could sing a silly song, like 'Happy Birthday everybody!'

Step 3: Classroom discussion – hero story

Ask your pupils to think of how the same lightshade might look if they were writing a story with a hero in it.

- There might be some kind of clue hidden under the lampshade – part of a map.
- The shade might be made from a map.

- The hero's enemy might have got to the room first and done something to the lamp. What kind of action adventure stories do you like?
- Who are your favourite heroes and heroines and what kind of opponents do they have? What kind of things do you have in these kinds of stories?

Imagine if you choose to have a teddy bear, doll or toy on the bed in the room?

- There might be some kind of message hidden in the teddy's clothing.
- The teddy might be dressed up as a superhero or in a safari outfit.
- You could use the teddy to give some kind of clue as to where the hero is going to end up.

Step 4: Classroom discussion – atmosphere

Imagine how the appearance of the main character in the story might contribute to the development of atmosphere.

- If this was a scary story, the character could think their big nose is a hideous deformity.
- If this was a funny story the character might have something distinctive about them – for example, they might have a nervous tick, a big nose, very hairy legs, or be short-sighted and the character could think his big nose is really a very attractive feature.
- If this was a story with a hero in it, the character might think their big nose is extremely distinguished or not care about it at all.

Step 5: Review of the task before pupils start writing

Having done the preliminary work, children can be reminded of the exercise. Take time to go over the following guidance with them.

Guidance

- The tricky part is that you are *only* to describe the room, and the things in it.
- Only *one* person enters the room or space. There are *no other people* in any of these scenes.
- The atmosphere that you create is going to tell your readers what kind of story this will be. Think about the weather outside the room, the lighting, the season, and how this can be used.
- You must use objects, furniture, evidence of hobbies and interests, clothes, and so on, to make sure that we know which kind of story this is going to be.
- Use your experiences – you will have some ideas from our discussion earlier or from sharing these ideas.
- There is no talking at all allowed but you can use written messages, notes on walls, on ceilings, in boxes, hidden, discovered, stuffed into places, if you like.

We should know from the description:

- Who is the person entering the room.
- What kind of story this is going to be.

Start writing!

You may find it helpful to post the following questions up on the interactive whiteboard (IWB) in case anyone gets stuck or needs some help.

Questions to help your writing

1 Imagine how many more aspects of your room can change, depending on which story you are going to tell. Think about:
   - the curtains
   - the old yew tree that has branches leaning against the window

- or maybe it is a cherry tree covered in blossom?
- the sky outside
- the bed covers
- the old wardrobe
- the colour or pattern of the wallpaper
- clues and objects that can be planted for use in the story later on.
2 Think about how the scene affects the five senses:
- describe what the room looks like
- what the room smells like
- what sounds can be heard
- what the various objects feel like to the main character
- can the main character touch something sticky and then taste it while they are in the room?

Step 6: Giving feedback

1 As pupils complete writing the exercise, they can share their work for feedback in pairs or groups.

2 The giving and receiving of feedback should follow guidelines in 4.5 *Giving feedback*. It is very important that each child who desires it should be given a chance to share their work and give feedback on the work of others.

3 We should know from the description:
- who is the person entering the room
- what kind of story this is going to be.
As pupils read each other's work, they could use this as a prompt to make sure that they understand the story the author is trying to tell.

4 It is sometimes useful with larger classes to get groups to choose their favourite example of the exercise to share with the whole class.

5 Children will understand the purpose of this exercise simply through reading each other's work and giving feedback.

Summary

Building atmosphere focuses on the potential offered by the use of the environment in storytelling, as well as the importance of character, the beginnings of 'planting and pay-off', together with story structure. An environment can add drama to events in a story and an environment can be used to help tell a story.

Through completing this exercise, children should now understand that the stories they liked the most, among the ones that they have read, will have been the stories based upon strong characters. Characters can be introduced through the ways that they interact with a given environment and the objects they find there. Characters can also be developed through their actions and activities

The exercise also shows how an object can be used to help tell a story, if it is planted in one scene and then seen again later in a different way. An object can also have its meaning and significance changed simply by changing its appearance in a different or later scene.

Finally, through discussion of different genres, we show how they usually work better if writers adhere to certain stylistic conventions

4.2 Sharing a room

Introduction

Sharing a room builds upon the potential offered by the use of the environment in storytelling that was begun in 4.1 *Building atmosphere*. It also helps pupils further develop a concept of how characters and their possessions and interests may change over time, and how conflict can impact an environment. This exercise again stresses the central importance of character, the beginnings of 'planting and pay-off', together with story structure.

Sharing a room introduces pupils to the following concepts:

- Characters can be introduced through the ways that they try to shape the environment where they live and the objects they choose to surround themselves with.

- An object can be used to deliver an entire story, if it is planted in one scene, and seen again later in a different way, and then shown in the final scene, changed again.
- An object can have its meaning and significance transformed simply through changing in its appearance in a later scene.
- A basic understanding of the conventions of three-act structure, because by following this template pupils will have produced a story in three parts (or acts).

This exercise reinforces the following:

- The best stories are based upon strong characters.
- The environment in which a story takes place can contribute to the drama.

Exercise 4.2: Sharing a room

Describe a bedroom where two people live. They can be brothers or sisters, a mother and father, a grandpa and grandchild, a boyfriend and girlfriend, two brownies or best friends, two young people sharing a room on a football training camp, two boys or girls sharing a room on an outdoor adventure week – it is up to you.
   Describe the room three times:

1   The two people are getting on really well.
2   There has been a fight between them.
3   One of the two people has moved out.

Step 1: Classroom discussion – personality clashes

The following questions about personality clashes and annoying people can be used to stimulate pupil discussion for *Sharing a room*.

- Do you get on really well with every member of your family?
- Is there anything that annoys you about someone in your family?

- Have you ever fallen out with a friend?
- What about when cousins, friends, relatives, grandparents come to stay?
- Ask 'Hands up everyone who gets on all the time with all of their family and never has an argument about anything?' (Usually no hands go up.)

Now get pupils to talk about the tiny things that can annoy us. You can give the pupils the examples listed and ask them if they can add to it:

- the toilet seat left up
- the yapping poodle pet
- the dog that is allowed to lick your aunt's plate clean after her meal
- the grandpa who picks out his pipe with a screw-driver and tips the waste onto the carpet
- the grumpy teenager who hogs the gameboy.

Step 2: Pair work – annoying habits

Get children to work in pairs to come up with a list of annoying habits or reasons that they may have argued with family members or friends. The pairs feed back to the class.

Tip

It can be useful at this point to enrich the range of examples generated, to separate cliques, for example the chess players, swots or class clowns, the four girls who are best friends and all love Barbies or the four boys who all have skateboards.

Step 3: Classroom discussion – 'revealing' characters

Pupils need to learn how to reveal characters, in writing, through their possessions. The following questions about how much you can tell about someone from the kinds of things they keep in their rooms can be used to initiate the second pupil discussion for *Sharing a room*.

- What kind of things can tell you who lives in a place and what kind of person they are?
- Does your granddad have false teeth on his bedside table?
- Does your mum have a picture of you as a baby on her bedside table?
- Does your big sister have a vampire book, or marathon running medals?
- Perhaps a big brother has a gameboy console, or a motorbike he is taking apart?
- Perhaps an aunt has a giant collection of wigs, or pink fluffy slippers?
- Does an uncle have a toy train collection?
- Or does a dad have a beer making kit?
- What do you have in your room?

Step 4: Pair work – favourite books

Pupils can work in pairs and ask each other, and report back to the group. They should come up with lists of favourite books like *Harry Potter*, pictures, posters of favourite sporting and TV stars, equipment for hobbies such as footballs, cricket gear, brownie uniforms, riding gear, or souvenirs, and they might be able to tell the stories behind these objects.

Step 5: Review of the task before pupils start writing

Having done the preliminary work, the children can be reminded of the exercise. Take time to go over the following guidance with them.

Guidance

- The tricky part is that you are *only* to describe the room, and the things in it.

- There are *no people* in any of these scenes.
- You should use objects, furniture, evidence of hobbies and interests, clothes, and so on, to describe the differences between the two people.
- Subtle changes should happen to the things in the room as the friendship between the two people goes wrong.
- Use your experiences – what objects do people keep with them, or display, that show us what kind of people they are? You will have some ideas from our discussion earlier or from sharing these ideas. You are free to borrow the description of someone else's granddad's nose-hair clippers if this would help your story.

Start writing!

You may find it helpful to post the following questions up on the IWB in case anyone gets stuck or needs some help.

Questions to help your writing

1   Who are these two people? How old are they? What do they look like? Are they pretty, handsome, vain (you can describe pictures pinned to walls or displayed in frames but remember there are *no people* in any of these scenes)?

2   We must know from the description of the room what happened between the two characters.

3   We will know who started the fight. It helps if you describe strong characters; some of these might include:
- A boy who leaves his muddy football gear around and a fussy brother who irons his clothes and collects catalogues of fashionable clothing.
- A girl who collects brownie badges and loves her brownie pack sharing with a sister who wears only black clothing and black make-up and reads vampire books.

- A boy who has big posters of scary monsters, big trucks and Voldemort is sharing a room with an aunt who has two shelves of hair products, three hairdryers, and DVDs of ballroom dancing.
- A granddad with false teeth and a hearing aid who shares a room with a grandson who likes really, really loud rock music and brings his motorbike into the room to repair it on granddad's neat bed.
- A girl with a giant collection of mini-teddies sharing a room with a boy who has a big collection of slugs and snails kept in glass jars.

4   We will know from your description what the fight was about.

5   We will know who moved out.

6   How long have they lived together? Eighty years? One week? What do they do for a living?

7   Are they intelligent? Have they dropped out of school or stayed on to university? Do they love school or do they play truant? Do they sneak out of school to go and play in the park?

8   What was the argument about? Who started it? How did they deal with it at first?

9   Who moved out? Why? Where did he/she go?

10   How did the other person, the one left behind, take it? Happy to be rid of them? Or sad?

11   Be selective with descriptions – pick the objects that define character.

12   For example, if a 7-year-old girl loves *High School Musical*, you do not need to list every one of the 40 items that she has, from dolls, to dance-mats, teddies to posters, that cover her side of the room. You could just say that 'Maddy's side of the room is completely covered in things that show her love of "High School Musical" – Troy Bolton's face smiles down from a poster on her Troy Bolton duvet cover and "High School Musical" paper tissues.' In this way you can make your description sharp and expressive, clear and selective.

13   Try to create a sense of discovery. Do not just list things haphazardly. You could write as if you have taken us, the reader, by the hand and you are guiding us around the room.

14 Remember the *Building atmosphere* exercise? What is the weather, the time of day, sounds and environment outside the room?

15 Can you *plant* any objects in the first scene, when the two people are getting on well, that can be used in later scenes?
  • That Troy Bolton poster – the Dr Who Poster – the pile of little teddies on the bed – what if someone has torn the poster in two or given Troy Bolton a pink bikini with a marker pen, or the slugs have escaped from their jar and are crawling all over the teddies?
  • Another example – if one girl has a Troy Bolton doll and her big sister is a fan of vampire stories, maybe in the first scene the Troy doll is lying happily in a little bed the girl has made; in the second scene he has a pair of black fangs drawn onto his face and perhaps fake blood poured on his smiling face on the bed cover; and in the final scene the side of the room covered in *High School Musical* objects has been stripped bare and the girl who was the big fan of Troy has moved out.

Step 6: Giving feedback

1 As pupils complete writing the exercise they can share their work for feedback in pairs or groups.

2 The giving and receiving of feedback should follow guidelines in 4.5 *Giving feedback*. It is very important that each child who desires it should be given a chance to share their work and give feedback on the work of others.

3 As pupils read each other's work, they could use the list below as a prompt to make sure that they understand the story the author is trying to tell.

4 It is sometimes useful with larger classes to get groups to choose their favourite example of the exercise to share with the whole class.

5 Children will get the purpose of this exercise simply through reading each other's work and giving feedback.

Feedback reminder

We should know from the description:

- Who these people are.
- What happened.
- Which one started the fight.
- What the fight was about.
- Who moved out.

Summary

The environment in which a character lives is a significant element of storytelling. Children will now understand that characters can be introduced through a description of their rooms and the objects they choose to surround themselves with.

Objects can be used to deliver an entire story, if they are planted in one scene, and seen again later in a different way, and then shown in the final scene, changed again. An object can also have its meaning and significance changed simply by altering its appearance in a different or later scene.

By following this template pupils will be able to produce a story in three parts (or acts) and thus they can begin to grasp a basic understanding of the conventions of the three-act structure. This exercise also reinforces the understanding that the best stories are based upon strong characters, and that the environment in which a story takes place can contribute to the drama.

Additionally, pupils will begin to understand the importance of preparation. During class discussion sessions, pupils will have worked as a group to discuss how family conflict can be used as a springboard for creativity. They will also have discussed how writers characterize people by their possessions and shared their personal experiences of conflict with family members during pair work.

Through this pupils will begin to learn that this writing exercise contains strict instructions that must be followed to achieve success. For example the fact that there will be no people at all in these descriptions, just the room that the people share, and the story will be told through the way that their room changes.

It empowers pupils to begin to develop a writer's ability to select elements and truths from their own lives to embellish and underpin their creative work. They will also develop powers of observation and description. In particular, pupils are encouraged to use economical detail – and through this they can build an understanding that a character can be revealed through the selection of just a few tiny pieces of information.

Writers need to learn how much can be left out, as well as how much needs to be left in, and this exercise enforces the use of ellipses, as the major action and conflict happens between the moments that the pupils describe.

The key role played by conflict in narrative is central to this exercise, which also develops the beginnings of classical narrative structure. This is because the template demands a story told in three parts – a set up, conflict and resolution – that mirrors the universal three-act structure.

This exercise offers a chance to discuss family dynamics, for example, how the children's own personalities interact with those of others, the development of methods of conflict resolution and perhaps offers children the chance to develop the beginnings of a form of acceptance of variety of human personality both within our lives and our schools.

The discussion can feed into other topic areas, but for the purposes of this creative writing exercise, we want the pupils to focus on conflict and the ways that it can be displayed.

The pupils are also offered the chance to explore the transformative power of fiction. They are beginning to get an understanding of the idea that the minute detail and irritations of daily life can be exploited to add great detail to build great stories.

The group and pair work enables pupils to share family stories (improving bonding, particularly in pupils who have been ostracized or left out, or even bullied) and, as pupils are encouraged to make suggestions as to how each other's stories should end, and in situations where pupils are using material that is autobiographical, they are in fact making suggestions as to how another pupil can resolve conflict within their own lives. Thus this exercise can build empathy and improve the ability of the children to empathize with the problems of others within their class.

4.3   Getting ready for a date

Introduction

Getting ready for a date builds upon the potential offered by the use of time-lapses in storytelling. It helps pupils further develop a concept of how characters and their possessions and interests may change over time (introduced in 4.1 *Building atmosphere* and 4.2 *Sharing a room*) and how conflict can impact an environment. This exercise again stresses the central importance of character and the beginnings of 'planting and pay-off', together with story structure.

Getting ready for a date introduces pupils to the following concepts:

- The fact that a story can be told through the actions of a character before and after a pivotal event, and that this event, perhaps one that determines the entire trajectory of the story, does not have to be described in detail, but can be powerfully indicated through its omission.
- In a similar way, the preparation for and aftermath of an event can be much more powerful than a description of the event itself.
- Props and clues can add rich layers of meaning to a story.
- A basic understanding of the conventions of three-act structure, because by following this template pupils will have produced a story in three parts (or acts).

This exercise reinforces the following concepts, which have been introduced in Exercises 4.1 and 4.2:

- An object can be used to deliver an entire story, if it is planted in one scene, and seen again later in a different way, and then shown in the final scene, changed again.
- An object can have its meaning and significance transformed simply through changing in its appearance in a later scene.
- The best stories are based upon strong characters.
- The environment in which a story takes place can contribute to the drama.

Exercise 4.3:   Getting ready for a date

Describe someone getting ready to go out on a date, and then returning from the date.

There are just two simple scenes, with only one character, in one room, with no talking. No exceptions: the character cannot talk to themselves or into a mobile phone.

Describe your character in the room two times:

1   Getting ready to go out. The scene ends when the character leaves the room.
2   Returning from the date.

We never see the person that your character went on the date with, nor do we hear their voice.

Step 1: Classroom discussion – annoying people

The following questions about personality clashes and annoying people can be used to stimulate pupil discussion for *Getting ready for a date*. Remind pupils that a date does not have to be romantic. It is just a promise to be somewhere – it could be an appointment at the dentist or a driving exam.

First, think about where your character is going on the date:

- Is it a first day at school?
- Playing football for England in the final of the World Cup?
- A job interview?
- A cricket, rugby or tennis final in which your main character is a key player?
- A ballet performance?
- A day at work in McDonald's, on a building site, cleaning toilets in an airport, or helping in a vet's office? Any other jobs that you know about?
- An appointment with a nasty doctor?

- An Olympic downhill ski race?
- A ride on a winning horse in the Epsom Derby?

And if the date is going to be romantic:

- Who is the date with?
- Is it a blind date?
- Boyfriend?
- Girlfriend?
- With someone they don't like?
- Someone they worship?
- Someone handsome? Ugly? Beautiful?
- What kind of date is it? Ballet? Dinner? Professional wrestling? In a big office building or in a giant football stadium?

Next, you need a clear picture of who this person is (the one going on a date). You are going to have to show us who this person is, by telling us the kinds of things they have in their room.

Step 2: Classroom discussion – who is your character?

This second list of questions will help you get started:

- What do we know about your character?
- What do they do for a living?
- If your character is a footballer, or a ballet dancer, what kind of things might they have around their room, that would let us know?
- If your character is going off for a day's work in McDonald's, what kind of clothes would such a person wear?
- What are their hobbies and interests?
- Are they in school or in college?
- Are they living on benefits?
- If your character was as old as your grandparents or great-grandparents, what kinds of things might very old people have in their rooms?
- How do they feel about themselves? Does your character think that they are extremely cool and wonderful, or extremely stupid

and unattractive? Or somewhere in-between? And how could you show us this?

- What kind of things do you think vain people do before they go out?
- And how would someone who felt sad, lonely or unattractive get ready for a date?
- How do they feel about the date – both before and after?

Step 3: Review of the task before pupils start writing

Having done the preliminary work, children can be reminded of the exercise. Take time to go over the following guidance with them.

Guidance

- The tricky part is that you are *only* to describe one person in a room, as they get ready for their date, and then when they get back from it.
- You must tell us what they look like, and how they act, as they get ready and when they get back from the date.
- You must use objects, furniture, evidence of hobbies and interests, clothes, and so on, to show us who this person is, and who the date is with, and where they are going.
- The way they act when they get back from the date will tell us how they feel about it.
- You cannot *tell* us what the character thinks, but you can *show* us through their actions.
- There is no talking at all in these scenes – they cannot talk to themselves or into a phone.

Start writing!

You may find it helpful to post the following questions up on the IWB in case anyone gets stuck or needs some help. However, if your pupils need more help before they start, or you believe they would benefit from more detailed preparation, the following questions can be discussed in pair work.

Questions to help your writing

1   You can show a character through their possessions. You do not have to list every item of make-up on a girl's dressing table to show that she is vain. Just choose three or four things that really sum it up – a giant mirror with light bulbs all around it, a wall covered in pictures of the girl in different poses, the heap of clothes that have been tried on, then rejected, all over the bed.

2   You can show a character through their physical appearance. How does your character look? People are not simply ugly or handsome. There are beautiful people who believe they are ugly; there are very ugly people who walk and talk as if they are beautiful, and as a result, others end up believing that they are beautiful. You can be beautiful but ugly on the inside, or ugly on the outside and beautiful on the inside, and so on. There is a wonderful illustration of this concept in the opening pages of Roald Dahl's novel, *The Twits*. Many of the characters in the *Shrek* films illustrate this point: Prince Charming is supposed to be gorgeous but is ugly on the inside; Shrek is meant to be ugly but is lovely on the inside.

   Often in feature films the evil characters are cast as less good looking than the heroes and heroines, but in your stories you do not have to follow these conventions.

3   Other tools that can be used include the following. Remember the *Building atmosphere* exercise – what time of day is it? Time of year? Sounds outside the room – traffic, howling wind, loud rock music, lawnmowers, screeching racing cars, galloping horses, ballet music? Sounds can be used, inside the room and outside the room, but not voices or dialogue.

4   Describe the main character so that we know who they are: tell us how he/she looks and walks, and give them a name. You can tell a lot about a person by their name. Can you imagine what the following people are like, just from their names?

Cindy, Vlad, Barry, Lara Croft, Gordon, Betsy, Fifi, Eric, Condoleezza, Paris, Zena, Boudicca, Peregrine, Bronwyn, Weezer, Dwayne, Clint, Jonny, Sherelle, Lucretia. (Pupils can provide more examples.)

Do you know people who are just like their names? Think of examples.

5   Plant and pay-off: can you *plant* any objects in the first scene of preparation that can be used in the second scene, when the character gets back from the date? For example, a famous footballer gets ready for an important match – he lays out a table with party food ready to celebrate his expected victory with his team after the match. When he returns from the match he has lost...he takes a look at the party food and...you might have some ideas as to what he could do with it.

Another example – a teenage girl is going on a date with a boy that she met on the Internet. She prints out his very handsome picture and draws hearts all around it, then pins it on her noticeboard before she goes out. When she comes back, we know things went very badly and the boy did not look at all as handsome as in the picture that he put on the Internet. What could the girl now do to the picture? What if she has an old dartboard in her room?

6   Props are the things we choose to have around us – remember 4.2 *Sharing a room*? Try to find and use one object that can reveal who your main character is. This might be tricky. If so, you can use some of the ideas below.

Can you get an idea of the character who might be the owner of the following:

- A Barbie doll in its original box
- A toy train set that takes up the whole room
- A Spiderman outfit
- A chess set with the pieces laid out and a guidebook to playing games with Russian grandmasters
- A collection of cute animal posters and fluffy teddies
- Star Wars light sabre
- Feather boas, sparkling clothes and a wardrobe overflowing with fashionable clothes
- A brownie or scout uniform covered in badges

- A collection of objects to celebrate a strong religious devotion
- A collection of mini-beasts like slugs and snails kept in glass containers
- A surfboard decorated with stickers from around the world
- Photos of a sporting hero.

7 If you are stuck, begin with props you know. Think about objects you might use to tell people about yourself. If your house was on fire, and your family members, pets and photo albums were all safe, what *one* object would you rescue from your room?

Step 4: Giving feedback

Feedback should follow guidelines laid out in Chapter 4.5. As pupils read each other's work, they can be reminded to ask themselves the following questions:

Feedback reminder

You should understand, as you read the work of other pupils:

- Who is the date with?
- Is it a blind date?
- What kind of date is it?
- Who is the person in the scene?
- How did they feel about the date – both before and after?
- What happened on the date?

Summary

Getting ready for a date builds upon the potential offered by the use of time-lapses in storytelling. This exercise again stresses the central importance of character, the beginnings of 'planting and pay-off', together with story structure.

Getting ready for a date helps pupils to develop an understanding of the power of omission and economy. Young writers can easily get lost in overwriting, in the mistaken belief that elaborate description creates a great story. The pace of the story will then flag. This exercise forces economy and teaches pupils that a scene that is left out can be more powerful than something that a writer takes the trouble to describe in great detail. Thus pupils are developing the ability to show us a character and avoid telling us about them (the 'show don't tell' rule).

In this exercise the main action happens outside the limits of what we are directly told – readers are forced to imagine what happened on the date, from the behaviour of the main character when he/she returns from the date. This puts our writers in the position of 'puppet-masters' – they have to control the reader's response to the material, and to do this they must gain a mastery of the use of clues, the foreshadowing of future events and the pay-off from past events, of props and physical communication.

A useful example of this is found in the *Harry Potter* books. We do not need to read 500 pages of the life of Harry before Hogwarts School, or later on, all about how horrible his summer holidays are with his Dursley relatives. If you just describe his bed in the cupboard under the stairs, that tells us all we need to know. Again, if you just show how Harry is left out of the dinner party in the second book, again that tells us all we need to know about Harry's summer holidays.

Pupils are beginning to learn the power of description, and the power of descriptions that they can generate themselves, to deliver strong, emotional stories. This understanding can help drive a desire to master a wider descriptive vocabulary and employ a more expansive range of descriptive language.

Pupils have enhanced their ability to describe characters and their emotions indirectly, through their actions and possessions. This can steer pupils away from storytelling through dialogue, or the delivery of plot directly through omniscient narration, which is the tendency of beginning writers.

Pupils are mastering an ability to evoke dramatic, emotional responses in a physical way, and they are learning that a high percentage of our communication as humans is non-verbal. Characters can tell us the whole of a very dramatic story – even a pivotal life-changing, vital moment in their lives – through their actions and activities in two simple scenes.

Thus through this exercise pupils will have begun to develop an ability to employ the fundamental narrative tools of 'planting and pay-off'.

Tip

If you want to reinforce the learning outcomes of this exercise, you can begin to talk about how stories work in three parts. This is called a three-act structure, and it exists to underpin almost all your pupils' favourite stories. This will be built upon in later classes but pupils have begun, in these early exercises, to incorporate the three-act structure into their own storytelling.

Your pupils will be able to add to the following examples of stories that are written in three parts:

- Little Red Riding Hood sets out for grandma's house.
- The wolf tries to convince her that he is grandma.
- Just as she is about to be eaten, the woodcutter arrives and kills the wolf (depending on which version you read).

In *The Three Little Pigs*, the Big Bad Wolf has *three* goes at blowing down the little pigs' homes.

Goldilocks goes to a house occupied by three bears, and then has three goes at taking over their belongings – eating their porridge, breaking their chairs, sleeping in their beds.

Jack goes up the Beanstalk three times – once he gets a bag of gold coins, the second time he gets a golden goose and the third time he gets a golden harp.

4.4 The character in the environment

Introduction

The character in the environment further develops the power of time-lapses in storytelling first encountered in 4.3 *Getting ready for a date*. It also helps pupils develop a concept of how the passage of time can impact both an environment and the characters who exist in it. This exercise again stresses the central importance of character, the beginnings of 'planting and pay-off', together with story structure.

The character in the environment introduces pupils to the following concepts:

- The fact that a story that takes place over a significant time frame, even a lifetime, can be told through the actions of a character between the most pivotal moments and that these events can be powerfully indicated through their omission.
- Props and clues planted throughout a story can have a significant role in plot development.
- Props, costume, environment and changes in the appearance of a character can add rich layers of meaning to a story.
- In a similar way, the preparation for and aftermath of an event can be much more powerful than a description of the event itself.
- A basic understanding of the conventions of the three-act structure, because by following this template pupils will have produced a story in three parts (or acts).

This exercise reinforces the following concepts that have been introduced in Exercises 4.1 and 4.2:

- An object can be used to deliver an entire story, if it is planted in one scene, and seen again later in a different way and then shown in the final scene, changed again.
- An object can have its meaning and significance transformed simply through changing in its appearance in a later scene.
- The best stories are based upon strong characters.
- The environment in which a story takes place can contribute to the drama.

Exercise 4.4: The character in the environment

Write three scenes. There is no talking in any of these scenes.

A character enters the same environment or place and meets another person three times.

Scene 1

The place is unfamiliar, mysterious to the character. The scene ends when he/she meets the other person. *They do not talk.*

Scene 2

The place seems familiar, friendly to the character. This time, the other person (same one) is expecting the character. The greeting is a happy one. No talking.

Scene 3

The place is deserted. There should be a feeling of sadness and nostalgia. The other person is not there this time. No talking by the main character.

Step 1: Classroom discussion – the new place

The following questions about personality clashes and annoying people can be used to stimulate pupil discussion for *The character in the environment*. Get your pupils to talk about their experiences the first time they went somewhere – how about:

- Their first day at school, or in their new class in the autumn
- The first time they went to ballet class, football club, brownies, scouts, a theme park, the zoo, or a riding stable
- The first time they went to see their grandma and grandpa
- The first time they went to a castle, beach, the doctor's surgery
- The first time they visited a relative in hospital
- The first time they saw their new house when they moved.

Step 2: Classroom discussion – losing things

Next, encourage your pupils to talk about their experiences of loss:

- Children might have lost contact with a person, a place or a house.
- Perhaps they have lost a treasured possession, or had to leave something behind?

- What did they lose?
- A pet, a toy, a house, a neighbourhood, a teacher, a friend?
- Did they do anything to show how they felt?
- Did anyone sulk?
- Was anyone naughty?
- What happened at the moment they realized they had lost this person, place or thing?

Step 3: Classroom discussion – change over time

Next, encourage your pupils to talk about the impact of time:

- How does a house, a person, or a place change over: 5 hours, 5 years, 20 years, 40 years, 100 years, 1000 years?
- What kind of clothes do people wear when they are: 7 years old, 14 years old, 30 years old, 60 years old, 90 years old?
- Apart from clothes, what are the main differences between very old people, middle-aged people and young children?
- What about their skin, or the way they walk?
- What does a brand new house look like?
- A house built in the 1960s?
- One built in Victorian times, or in Tudor times?
- In Norman times, or in the Stone Age?
- What does a house look like if it has been abandoned or neglected?
- How do you know if a house is brand new, or if it is 300 years old?
- Can you look into the future and work out how to show that a character, place, house or area might age over time?
- Pupils may have experienced history projects where they saw the kind of clothes their grandparents or great-grandparents used to wear, or covered the Second World War, or the Tudors.

Step 4: Classroom discussion – favourite authors

The following examples from fiction and film can be used if you feel pupils would benefit from finding out about how the techniques used in this exercise are employed by some of their favourite authors. Pupils can be encouraged to add their own examples.

Examples from fiction and film

- Remember how Harry Potter's parents helped to save his life during the fight with Voldemort? This scene is not described in detail. The horror of it is shown in the lightning scar on Harry's forehead, and the fact that Harry is left an orphan. J.K. Rowling resists telling us the detail of this pivotal moment, or the whole series of events leading up to Harry's escape from Voldemort as a baby. From the very start of the series the author provides her readers with just enough information so that they can fill in the gaps. Economy is a crucial tool in the good writer's arsenal and our pupils will be able to use this throughout their written work.
- Shrek had some bad experiences when he tried to live among normal people, and these experiences seem to have led to his strong desire to live alone. We are not told every detail about what happened – we just see him nailing a sign up that states 'Keep Out' in the opening scene of the film, and this tells us all we need to know.
- In *The Lady and the Tramp*, we do not have the whole story about why Tramp does not live with people, or even about the lives of the other dogs in the pound.
- In *Cinderella*, we do not get great detail about what her life was like before she started working as a scullery maid for the Ugly Sisters and her stepmother.

Tip

At this point teachers can reference any visits to historical places with school, or that the children have experienced themselves. For example, if pupils have covered the evacuations of school children during the Second World War, they may use this exercise to show a girl from the city arriving at a farm for the very first time, coming back as a grown woman, and then perhaps returning as an old woman, to find the farm very changed.

The National Curriculum in the UK ensures that all primary children cover the story of the Blitz and the evacuation of young children to the countryside. This means that they have covered sometimes disturbing stories about children being bombed, losing parents and even their own lives. Fiction work with this historical information can give children 'ownership' over difficult information, a more layered, nuanced comprehension and their own feeling of control over it.

These exercises could easily be fine-tuned to really help children understand issues raised by the kind of history covered by different curricula worldwide.

This is a good example of the potential of the creative writing classes to draw upon and cross-fertilize and thus enrich other areas of the curriculum.

Fans of children's television history shows, like the BBC's *Horrible Histories*, will be able to draw upon these resources.

Pupils may decide to use an event from history as inspiration for the change of mood between the three scenes.

Step 5: Review of the task before pupils start writing

Having done the preliminary work, children can be reminded of the exercise. Take time to go over the following guidance with them.

Guidance

- Describe only what your readers could see and hear if they were there. If you write out the thoughts of your character you are explaining the story to us rather than telling us the story. This gets boring. Your readers want to work it out for themselves.
- If you begin to use conversation at this stage, between your characters, there is a risk that you will just tell us everything you think we need to know, rather than letting us, the readers, find out.
- You are being forced to rely upon your powers of description. The way you describe the main character, how they look, walk, run or crawl, throw themselves to the ground in anger, collapse with grief,

or do a dance of victory, will tell your readers what they need to know.

- Give your character a name – names are an important tool in telling us who a person is. (There is a note about this in 4.3 *Getting ready for a date.*)

Start writing!

You may find it helpful to post the following questions up on the IWB in case anyone gets stuck or needs some help.

Questions to help your writing

Scene 1

1 You need to have a strong character in mind as you write the scenes. *Who is your character?* How old are they? Why are they coming to this place? What do they expect to find? What do they think about it – are they scared, happy, looking forward to it?
2 You need to have a story in mind as you write the scenes. Show how the story develops in three scenes. The most important parts of the story happen between the scenes that you describe, and your readers are going to be forced to work this out for themselves, from the clues you are giving them.
3 Pupils might want to 'plant' some object in the first scene that can be used in the second and third scenes. Try to find a prop that reveals character. (Remember the *Sharing a room* exercise'?)
4 This 'planted' object can have great meaning in the last scene:
   - a bunch of flowers in the second scene is now dried up and wilted
   - a pair of ballet shoes given earlier is now worn out and discovered in a bin
   - a forgotten gas mask is found in a trunk

   and so on.

Scene 2

Your main character returns:

- How has the place changed?
- How has the main character changed? Are they more confident now? Or more nervous?
- What are they doing there again?
- What happened?
- How has this affected the character?
- What has happened to the place?

Scene 3

1 The place has changed since scene 2, now that the second character is no longer there – tell us how, exactly?
2 How does your main character react, physically, to this loss:
    - slumped, slouched, skipping with joy, collapse on the floor
    - weeping, rushing around stealing fixtures and fittings
    - gobbling the box of chocolates and the stale cake left behind
    - opening their own ballet/football/riding school, or setting fire to it?

    Remember, you cannot cheat by having your character tell a friend on their mobile phone, or suddenly start talking to themselves. There is no talking in this scene, at all.
3 How has your main character changed since the second scene?
    - Has the child become an adult, or even a very old man or woman?
    - Are they richer, poorer, healthier, happier, since scene 2?
    - How can you show this?
4 Has the second character left behind any clues as to their whereabouts? This could include:
    - memorial cards
    - bunches of flowers
    - an arrest warrant
    - a farewell card
    - a box of ashes
    - an invitation to a funeral

- a receipt for plane tickets to Brazil
- a box of final belongings put in a cardboard box by hospice staff?

Or can we just tell by the way that all the animals are gone, the farmhouse has broken windows and no roof, that the farmer has died or given up?

5   Try to be clear about the story you have told. Do you think your readers can work out what has happened? What has gone on between the scenes?

6   Can you think of physical changes that can show us what happened between the scenes? How much time has passed? Five hours? Or five years? Five hundred years? What changes between the scenes and what stays the same?

7   Remember to use the atmosphere, time of day, weather, and wear and tear to help create telling changes in the environment. The way the character walks, looks around and so on, will tell your readers about how he/she has aged or changed. Plant and pay-off can also be very useful.

Step 6: Giving feedback

Feedback should follow guidelines laid out in Chapter 4.5. As pupils read each other's work they can be reminded to ask themselves the following questions.

Feedback reminder

You should understand, as you read the work of other pupils:

- Who is the main character?
- Who do they meet during the first scene and why is this important to them?
- What has happened between the first scene and the second – how much time has passed?

- What has happened by the end?
- What happened to the second character and how does your main character feel about this?

Summary

The character in the environment helps pupils further develop a concept of how to evoke the passage of time both upon an environment and the characters who exist within it. This exercise stresses the central importance of character and the beginnings of 'planting and pay-off', together with story structure.

This exercise reinforces the understanding, developed in earlier work, that the dramatic moments of a story can happen between the key moments described. Your pupils will learn to focus in on pivotal 'hot' emotional moments, the moments when change occurs in characters, as these moments can be all that is needed to tell a story covering a lifetime (or even longer)!

It encourages a form of group-bonding and safety. As your pupils share stories of loss and change they can begin to get an understanding that the greatest or best storytelling is dependent upon the sharing of some form of emotional truth.

The sharing of stories of loss by children at this stage is central to the act of creative writing and the successful construction of such writing. This will in turn foster a group dynamic that supports the sharing of emotion and vulnerability will help encourage the supportive giving of feedback and ideas. Without constructive feedback from peers, your pupils will miss out on one of the most useful and transferable skills that a writing class can deliver.

It must be emphasized that this exercise is about learning to tap personal experience, powers of observation and universal emotion to create fiction. Students are doing this work to acquire a basic tool of writing. This is not therapy and the preparatory work is only there to ensure the writing is powerful.

Good writing must move us, emotionally. Writers, at their best, can be like puppet-masters, who know exactly how to make their characters display emotion, and how to generate an emotional response from a reader.

Your pupils are learning the art of alchemy – the writer's talent to transform the everyday, sometimes painful or mundane into something emotionally gripping and affective.

The preparatory work reinforces the learning in earlier exercises of writing as a craft rather than as a gift given only to the lucky few. Pupils are beginning to learn that writing fiction can provide them with a greater engagement with historical fact. Early discussion in pairs or small groups reinforces confidence in the most shy or reluctant pupils because they are being asked to talk about things that have happened to everyone.

This exercise also deals with loss – a crucial theme in narrative composition. In every story, at some point, the main character will suffer some sort of loss or setback. Thus with this exercise children can experiment with, perhaps master and certainly become familiar with one of the most fundamental components of good storytelling.

Your pupils will gain experience of the fact that very often a story happens between the moments that are actually described. An accomplished writer knows that readers enjoy the challenge of creating the precise detail or 'backstory' about a character or scene for themselves. Young writers may believe that to create interesting work, they need to include every word they can locate to paint a character or scene. However, the best work will depend more upon the skilful 'drip-feeding' of only the most essential, telling detail.

4.5   Giving feedback

Introduction

Feedback builds upon the potential offered for the development and encouragement of children's writing through peer review. It is designed to deliver a wide range of social and literary skills.

This section has important information about how to encourage your pupils to give constructive feedback upon each other's work. This section needs to be read carefully as it is the key to running a successful creative writing class. The ability to give constructive feedback will enrich not only your pupils' writing but also their ability to contribute constructively in a multitude of group work settings.

Writing, literacy and social skills

The feedback exercise will help pupils to develop the following:

- An acute awareness of what works in writing and what does not work.
- Confidence in reading the handwriting of others, and confidence in reading out loud.
- The potentially very empowering experience of engaging for once with the point of view of the teacher. This is because pupils are being asked to think about why some stories work and why others are not as successful, thus pupils are in a position to reinforce the learning outcomes established through the exercises.
- Group empathy and cohesion.
- As the structure given for feedback forces pupils to find something to like about each piece of work, pupils will begin to understand the concept that writing is rewriting, and become more adept at locating what works and what needs to be improved in their own work.
- Positive peer feedback will improve confidence and plant the desire to write better.
- When hearing peers stumble over poorly expressed or badly written work, pupils will be provided with a concrete incentive to improve their own writing in terms of grammar and presentation.
- Pupils are being asked to engage critically, rather than passively, with a piece of writing, at the point of creation.

Exercise 4.5:   Giving feedback

1   Pupils complete any writing exercise in this book.
2   They then pass their completed exercise along to the pupil sitting next to them. In this way each pupil gets a copy of another pupil's work to read.
3   Pupils read each other's work and begin to give each other feedback.

Tip

You need to be aware of the vulnerability of pupils sharing creative work. Children in a creative writing class will be extremely motivated by the idea that their work is to be shared with an audience of their peers. This will be one of the few times during their education that they can receive positive feedback for work that has been generated from their own imaginations, work in which they have an emotional investment and direct creative ownership.

Children may feel that the writing is not only personal to them, but also intrinsically a part of them – and thus the exposure of this writing to a classroom audience needs to be handled with care. Following these guidelines will make the experience of giving and receiving feedback one of the most enjoyable and inspirational moments in their writing coursework.

In the creative writing classroom, we learn nothing if we are given bland comments and kindness. Feedback is useful only when it is specific and includes suggestions as to how we might improve our writing, or make it more effective. Yet inexperienced writers may feel they have to give only positive feedback because they are nervous about how their own writing may be received, or because they want to be kind.

The **framework for giving feedback** and the **golden crock**, described below, have been designed to create a classroom environment where the skilful use of feedback can be nurtured. The framework for giving feedback can be used alongside the golden crock.

Framework for giving feedback

Step 1: The work to be critiqued is read out loud

The piece of writing can be read out loud within smaller groups or in pairs. During feedback sessions small groups must be patrolled and monitored, and good feedback practice praised and shared with the larger class.

The teacher's presence, encouragement and awareness of the dialogue that pupils are engaged in will ensure that creative work is developed in a secure, safe environment.

- If the handwriting is clear enough, this is best done by a child who was not the author.
- This way pupils can get an idea of what their writing sounds like.
- Errors will often make the reader stumble, and so pupils can be inspired to improve their spelling and the clarity of their handwriting – children will want their work to be understood.
- Teachers can use their own judgement as to whether or not pupils' writing will be clear enough to be read out, and whether or not pupils are ready for this.

Step 2: The plot is summed up

Another way to overcome resistance to giving feedback is to have one pupil (not the author) sum up what they think happened in the story. This means that pupils can hear immediately if their story has not been understood, or if their goals for the story have not been realized. For example, if the other pupils think that Cinderella was an ugly sister whose foot did not fit into the little shoe, the author might be able to work out ways to make it clear that the shoe did fit Cinderella and she was not ugly.

Suggestions can also be made at this point, as to how the story can be made more accessible.

Step 3: Group members should say something that they liked about the work

Pupils can be asked to consider:

- What are the main strengths of the piece?
- Feedback can be phrased as 'The part of the story we liked the most is when this or that happened.'

Step 4: Group members should suggest ways the story could be improved

- Pupils can suggest elements of the story that they would like to find out more about, for example, exactly how the witch looks, or how old the main character is.

- Suggestions can be made as to how the author could address any problems raised during earlier discussion, for example, how the plot could be made simpler.

Step 5: The author of a piece can ask for feedback

- For example, the author can ask others if there was anything they did not understand.
- Or if a part of the story was hard work, or was very important, or there is something that they really worked hard at, they can ask others if they thought this worked.

Tip

A further option, if time allows, could be for each group to subsequently give feedback to the whole class. Time pressure might dictate that the group select a favourite story to talk about. In this way pupils might have their story summed up by another group member to the whole class, for example: 'Bella's story was about a pirate who wanted to get the other half of the map leading to the treasure. The mean pirate was sitting in a bar playing cards and the good pirate had to creep up without being seen. We liked how hard it was for the good pirate and we wanted to find out more about what they all looked like.'

The golden crock

To overcome pupil resistance to giving constructive feedback, the golden crock is useful. The golden crock removes responsibility for delivering the criticism from your pupils and places it with the crock, or with the teacher enforcing its use. This frees the pupils from awkwardness, guilt and shyness they may feel in having to criticize the work of their peers.

Step 1: Introduce the 'crocks' to your pupils

Each small group of students working together and providing feedback will need a small teacup, preferably golden or yellow; paper cups also work well. The name 'golden crock' can be written on the cup. For a class of thirty pupils, divided into six groups, you would need six golden crocks.

Give one pupil at each table a cup. Tell the whole class that the holder of the 'golden crock' is the one who is going to be forced to come up with an idea that could improve the story that has been read out.

Step 2: Pupils start to use the crocks

After each piece of work has been critiqued, the crock rotates along to the next pupil, with the aim that every student should have the chance to deliver constructive criticism.

- No suggestion can be dismissed as 'stupid' or 'ridiculous'.
- The story's author can just say 'Thank you for your idea' to the crock holder.

You should patrol your groups of pupils as they read each other's work and enforce the use of the crock. For example, if a crock-holder is overheard giving lavish praise, the teacher can urge them to keep going until they can find a way to improve the story, and thus do 'as the crock bids'.

Your pupils may sometimes be in awe of each other's work and convinced that it is beyond improvement. They may want to be kind to make sure that their own work is praised. To help pupils see how the golden crock works, you can add your own ridiculous suggestions to the following two examples.

Examples from fiction and film

- I do not like the fact that the Wile E. Coyote is always tortured by the Road Runner. If I could advise the writer, I would suggest that we see the Coyote eating delicious Roasted Road Runner in one episode.
- I do not like the fact that the Big Bad Wolf ends up in a boiling pot of water in the house of the pig that built his house with bricks. Why not have the Wolf grab the pig and stick him into the pot of water, and eat him?

It does not matter that the two suggestions are quite silly and not useful. It might give the author an idea for a new story. As a pupil thinks over the suggestions, however silly they might seem, they might come up with their own, perfect way to improve their story.

A writer might just say 'Thank you for your suggestion' and not use the idea. But at least we followed the rules of the golden crock and came up with a suggestion. And that is what all your pupils must learn to do.

Tip

- To balance out the golden crock, stuffed 'love hearts' can be given to groups. The 'love heart' can also be made from heart-shaped pieces of paper. The 'love heart' is effective but not often necessary, as pupils' first instinct is to give praise to each other.
- You can give the love heart to a pupil sitting on the opposite side of the table to the holder of the crock.
- The holder of the love heart, which also rotates round each group, is the one who must come up with something very kind and loving to say about the piece of writing.

Summary

Through the *Giving feedback* exercise your pupils will get to hear how a secondary audience comprehends their story. If their fellow pupils' interpretation differs greatly from the author's intention, then the author will learn in a very immediate way areas in which their writing is not clear and get a good idea of what needs to be done to improve their work. Pupils are thus developing and strengthening their own comprehension skills.

Pupils will learn about the kinds of detail that readers value, and work out innovative ways to deliver this. For example, if one of Bella's pirates is really evil, she needs to find ways to let her readers get this, through the way he plays cards, or the weapons he is carrying.

This exercise enables pupils to develop the ability to add a layer of sophisticated description to a story, and to understand that description does not simply sit there for decorative effect, but in good storytelling description is there for a purpose – to make sure that readers understand the narrative.

Pupils are learning to give and receive constructive criticism upon each other's work. Developing suggestions as to what could be improved about another's story enhances their own storytelling skills, builds independence in developing solutions to their own storytelling problems, and develops confidence. The ability to give and receive criticism is an essential tool for future progress in writing and in every area of life and education.

Use of these techniques will ensure that pupils master an essential writing tool – thinking up ways that their own and others' work can be improved. As pupils address areas of concern – the need for more description, for more clues, for a clearer plot – they are gaining practical experience of the building blocks of fine writing.

The sharing of feedback will help beginning writers who can be anxious that their first efforts at writing should be as polished as the authors that they admire. Children will begin to develop an understanding that writing is a craft that can be learned and that writers do not sit awaiting divine inspiration to strike from above and direct their brain to create fabulous prose. Writing is rewriting. Pupils can learn that the stories they love so very well have been crafted, drafted, sweated over, polished and rewritten over and over again before they were fit for publication.

Although we all love being praised, particularly after sharing personal, creative work, your pupils will really appreciate being allowed to hear about the parts that do not work, and hearing suggestions as to how to improve their work.

5 Story building

5.1 The object and the obstacle

Introduction

The object and the obstacle focuses on the development of a strongly dramatic scene between two characters. It also reinforces elements of storytelling covered in Chapter 4, including the importance of character, the use of 'planting and pay-off', together with story structure.

It introduces pupils to the following concepts:

- The drama can be developed around one obstacle and a struggle for its possession.
- A story can be told through three major actions or dramatic moments.
- Each pivotal moment should build from a previous one.
- The frustration of the hero's desires is a fundamental component of all good storytelling.

Exercise 5.1: The object and the obstacle

Write one short half page.

You are writing a short scene with people in it but they cannot talk.

One character is going to try to get something from the other character.

As the story begins, the *opponent* has the object that the *main character* wants.

The *main character* tries two or three times to get the object from the *opponent*. Each one fails.

At last, growing desperate, the *main character* makes one more try. Does she/he succeed or fail? Can you think of a twist for the ending?

Step 1: Classroom discussion – defining the desire

You can get your pupils to talk about objects and things that other family members have, that they want or need. There must have been times when your pupils have desperately wanted something, and this can help them to come up with some ideas for what their main character could want.

For example:

- An older brother or sister may have a toy or book that they will not share.
- A friend may have a computer game that they want and the friend will not share it.
- It might be some kind of food, sporting equipment or clothing.

Step 2: Pair work – pester power

Children can break into pairs to come up with some ideas for what exactly their character might want. They can also discuss their own 'pester power' talents for getting what they want. The children can report back to small groups regarding the ideas they generated in pair work.

Step 3: Classroom discussion – making the obstacle tricky

Your pupils should be able to contribute to the following list of examples that explain why the obstacle is important, and the kinds of obstacles that are used in their favourite stories. Usually the main character's opponent is also a very strong character.

Examples from fiction and film

- In *Harry Potter and the Philosopher's Stone*, Harry wants to get his letter from Hogwarts, but his uncle seals up the letterbox and takes him to a remote lighthouse.
- In *Pirates of the Caribbean*, the bad pirates of the Black Pearl want to collect the last piece of enchanted Aztec gold coin that the heroine, Elizabeth, wears round her neck as a pendant.
- In *Goldilocks and the Three Bears*, Goldilocks wants food and a comfy bed.
- In *The Three Little Pigs*, the pigs all want cosy homes that are safe from the Big Bad Wolf.
- In *Cinderella*, the kitchen girl wants a dress to go to the ball.
- In *Little Red Riding Hood*, the girl wants to deliver her basket to grandma.
- In *Hansel and Gretel*, the children want to avoid being eaten by the Witch.
- In many *Winnie the Pooh* stories, Winnie the Pooh wants to steal honey and the bees do not want to let him have it.
- In *Harry Potter and the Chamber of Secrets*, Harry wants an ingredient for a potion but he must get it from the room of the potion's master, Snape, who is his opponent.
- The crocodile wants to eat the rest of Captain Hook in *Peter Pan*, but his efforts keep being frustrated.
- Many *Tom and Jerry* cartoons are based upon this idea, together with *Road Runner*, and even *Charlie and Lola* stories.

This is one of the most powerful tools of storytelling: the frustration of the hero's desires is a fundamental component of every worthwhile story. If the hero or heroine could get what they wanted easily, there would be no story at all. For example: Shrek would still be alone in his swamp; Harry Potter would get rid of Voldemort in the first book and the other six would never have been written; Little Red Riding Hood would have got the basket to grandma with no problem.

No problem means no story!

Step 4: Pair work – a strong opponent

Children can now be set the next task: they can work in (preferably new) pairs to decide upon a suitable opponent to their main character. It can be anyone they like: a character they know, one they have made up, or one they could borrow from a story or film that they like, or one borrowed from someone else in class, or from an earlier exercise.

You can suggest some ideas if your pupils get stuck:

- What if a child needs his granddad's false teeth to make a scarecrow but his granddad wants to eat his dinner?
- How does Snape feel about letting Harry Potter have his potion ingredients? You need to have an opponent who feels strongly and is going to put up a good fight against your main character.
- The wolf is very hungry and wants to eat Little Red Riding Hood so much that he is prepared to dress up as grandma. How does the wolf feel about the girl?

The children can now report back to smaller groups the results of their work.

Step 5: Review of the task before pupils start writing

Having done the preliminary work, the children can be reminded of the exercise. Take time to go over the following guidance with them.

Guidance

- The tricky part is that you are *only* to describe two people in one place.
- They cannot talk.

- Think of a reason why they cannot talk: they could be at a loud rock concert, at the theatre, in a library, at a wedding, a funeral, in a religious service; they could be animals or very young children who cannot talk yet.
- Tell us what they look like, and how they act, as one character tries to get something from the other.
- As the story begins, the *opponent* has the object that the *main character* wants.
- You must use objects, furniture, evidence of hobbies and interests, clothes, and so on, to show us who these characters are.
- And why the main character needs the object.
- The main character tries two or three times to get the object from the opponent. Each one fails.
- At last, growing desperate, the main character makes one more try. Does she/he succeed or fail? Can you think of a twist for the ending?
- You cannot *tell* us what the character thinks, but you can *show* us through their actions.

Start writing!

Pupils should be given time to complete the exercise and then share their work and provide feedback.

You may find it helpful to post the following questions up on the IWB in case anyone gets stuck or needs some help.

Questions to help your writing

Choose a *main character.* Anybody you want. You can use a character from any of the earlier exercises if you like, or a character that someone in your class has told you about. Give them a name.

Choose something:

- a box of sweets
- a magician's wand

- a book
- a can of pop
- a tray of freshly baked buns
- a potion
- some treasure
- a clue
- a magic spell
- an eyeball
- a model aeroplane
- a pair of roller skates
- a vial of blood
- a cricket bat
- a bag of guinea-pig food
- a saddle for a pony
- a computer game
- a piece of clothing.

It has to be something that this person wants or needs.

Work out for yourself reasons why he/she needs it so badly.

You don't have to reveal to the readers right at the start why your main character needs this thing so very badly. This will be shown by the end.

However, it must be clear to your readers that your main character *wants* it.

Remember:

- The *opponent* may or may not be aware that the *main character* wants the object (your choice)
- The *opponent* may or may not even be aware of the presence of the object or its value to anyone (your option)
- The *main character* and the *opponent* may or may not know each other (your choice).

You can use ideas that you developed in the *Building atmosphere, Sharing a room, The character in the environment* and *Getting ready for a date* exercises in this work.

- Where are your characters?

- What is the atmosphere?
- Can we tell anything about them from what they own, wear, or are decorated with?

Step 6: Giving feedback

Feedback should follow guidelines laid out in Chapter 4.5. As pupils read each other's work, they can be reminded to ask themselves the following questions.

Feedback reminder

You should understand, as you read the work of other pupils:

- Who is the main character?
- Why do they want the object?
- Why does their opponent make it difficult for them to get it?
- How does your main character feel about the object – both before and after the scene?
- What happened in the end – who got the object in the end?

Summary

In this exercise the writing begins with the sharing of ideas. The simple act of getting some ideas down on the page is the beginning of good writing practice. The writing should be a story about two characters engaged in a struggle for possession of something of value, and the work that they have just completed – the struggle to locate the perfect opponent, to add to the agony of their main character – is the kind of work that is fundamental to the work of all the authors that they know and love.

Within storytelling for novels and films, characters must have a desire, a *goal*, they must want some thing – and meet obstacles that get in the way of them achieving their desire. Without obstacles there would be no story. To reinforce earlier discussion, consider the following examples.

> **Examples from fiction and film**
>
> - If Harry Potter went to Hogwarts with no problem, had a great time and there was no Voldemort in the way, you would have no story.
> - If Little Red Riding Hood could deliver the basket to her grandma by walking through a leafy wood safely, there would be no story.
> - If the Three Little Pigs could build houses that would be safe from wolves, again, no story.
> - If Romeo could marry Juliet with both families' happy approval, there would be no play.

You can extend the following examples and let children work out what the *main goals* of their favourite characters are.

Through this preparatory exercise children can begin to unpick the major plot points of their own favourite stories, and thus begin taking ownership of the material. They will begin to understand that all great stories are intricately structured and plotted, and that their authors use a palette of techniques that the children themselves can adopt, not only for this particular exercise, but also in all kinds of writing.

The exercise that the pupils have just gone through in class, creatively thinking up obstacles and coming up with solutions, is something that their favourite authors do every working day of their lives. Through doing this exercise they have begun to develop skills used by professional working writers. For example, Shrek wants to be alone – yet his swamp is invaded by fairy tale creatures. In *Toy Story*, the cowboy wants to be the boy's favourite toy again. In *Pirates of the Caribbean*, Jack Sparrow wants to get a ship.

Someone had to think up these problems. That was the writer, and your pupils have just learned not only how to create their own obstacles, but also a fundamental building block of storytelling.

Even in primary school, children may have been read stories and started to interpret them within the confines of literary interpretation (in part because this will probably be the way that their teachers have traditionally encountered literature). However, through these creative writing exercises children get the chance to comprehend literature from the point of view of the author, and not the critic, and through this can begin to view texts as a rich toolkit of techniques to be sampled and exploited to enrich their own writing.

5.2 Persuasion: unexpected arrival

Introduction

Persuasion: unexpected arrival focuses on the development of a strongly dramatic scene between two main characters. It also reinforces elements of storytelling covered in Chapter 4 including the importance of character, the use of 'planting and pay-off', together with story structure.

It introduces pupils to the following concepts:

- The drama of a story can be developed around one pivotal moment.
- Dialogue has multiple functions within a story: it can be used to help us understand characters, as well as inform us about what is going on.
- A story can be told through three major actions or dramatic moments.

The exercise builds upon work covered in 5.1 *The object and the obstacle* by reinforcing the fact that:

- Each pivotal moment should build from a previous one.
- The frustration of the hero's desires is a fundamental component of all good storytelling.

Exercise 5.2: Persuasion: unexpected arrival

Your main character is expecting someone. A third, totally unexpected person arrives. This person is annoying, gets in the way, and has come at the wrong time: use whatever you can think of to make the main character really stressed.

Your main character must now get rid of the unexpected person before the other (expected) person arrives.

Dialogue is allowed.

Step 1: Classroom discussion – annoying people

Encourage your pupils to talk about the most annoying member of their families, or the most annoying person that they have come across.

- What makes this person so very annoying?
- Have you ever tried to avoid this person?
- Is the annoying person persistent?

Try to work out some situation that you would not want your annoying person to show up for; this might include something like the following:

- Your awful Aunty Joyce, who plays the piano and sings horribly whenever she can, has invited herself to your birthday party and is going to ruin it. You are desperate to get rid of her, and she is determined to stay.
- Your big sister catches you dressing up in her favourite outfit, that you have 'borrowed' (without her permission) because it really suits you and you need to wear it to a great party. Imagine how hard it would be to get rid of your sister and pretend you are not wearing it to any party.
- You are just about to play the most difficult football game of your life against the toughest team in the area, when your horrible uncle shows up in his Arsenal shirt, stands on the sideline of the pitch and attacks the referee.
- Imagine how hard it might be to get rid of this awful uncle, if the uncle believed you were going to be the next Wayne Rooney and believed you needed his support to do this? And what if some scouts for Chelsea were expected that day – but if they see your uncle, in his Arsenal shirt, hitting the referee, you know it will be all over for you?
- Could religious, cultural or social beliefs make any of your situations more stressful? What if the whole family sit down for a meal that marks an important date in their religion (Christmas, Yom Kippur, Diwali, Ramadan) and the long lost son or daughter turns up and ridicules their beliefs, just before their religious leader is due to arrive?

- What if your family were all very anti-religious, and one aunty has converted to become an evangelical Christian, Muslim, Hindu, Jain, Jew (whatever you can imagine would create the biggest problem) and arrives at the house with a bible, Koran, torah, other holy book or a tambourine to pray over all of you, just before you are about to start the biggest rave the street has ever seen?

There are many examples of this kind of unexpected arrival scene in books and films. A perfect example can be found in one of the *Harry Potter* books, where the Dursleys are expecting very important guests for dinner, have created a very fancy dinner, and have rehearsed what they are going to say and do with the guests. Harry has been banned to his room and told that nothing magical can happen. Then Dobby, a house-elf who serves the Malfoy family, arrives and causes mayhem. Harry tries, over and over, to get rid of Dobby before the Dursleys can find out.

Once children have completed this exercise they will be able to identify scenes like these in many other texts.

Step 2: Pair work – character work

Your pupils must know who their characters are. (More detailed work on characters will be done in 8.1 *Character profiles*.)

Pupils also need to work out the relationship the two characters have. These people have known each other for some time; they have a history together. Your pupils could consider writing a short character profile on each character (as preparation, not to be read in class).

Step 3: Group work – dialogue

It is very easy to depend too heavily upon dialogue to deliver narrative, and this is why characterization, description and action have been concentrated on during the early exercises.

The beginning writer often believes that dialogue is the most obvious and simple way to deliver the plot. Favourite stories may be remembered in terms of wonderful, pithy lines of dialogue – what is not remembered is the backdrop developed by the author, against which those lines were spoken, and without which dialogue is meaningless.

Dialogue shorn of supporting background information and plot is sometimes used in daytime soap operas and badly written stories, to enable difficult plot lines to be delivered quickly. The problems with an over-reliance upon dialogue can be discussed with children. What is the problem with the example (below)?

> A man accuses his wife of betraying him:
> 'But Cheryl! Do you mean to say that the twins you are carrying are not mine? Was that man you have been seeing, Fred, the footballer, the real father of the twins? Oh, how could you do this to me? I am so gutted?! This must have been going on since the big staff party at Christmas – when you said you felt ill – and I remember, Fred offered to drive you home – oh no, don't tell me that was when … when you first fell in love with Fred?'

Pupils might be aware of the over-use of clunking dialogue like this in texts that they have encountered.

A lot of information is carried in the dialogue above.

- Can you think of any other ways that the information delivered through this speech, could be shown?
- How do you show that someone is pregnant with twins?
- How could you show readers that a woman is in love with another man?

Pupils can now think of actions that the characters might have, things they might do, props they might use, that would tell us more about the plot than this dialogue, and at the same time, let us know more about the characters and their motivations, and thus become more interesting?

Now that the exercises use dialogue, it is possible, depending upon the children's level of confidence, to 'cast' stories and have the dialogue read out, either within pairs, or groups, or to the whole class, depending upon levels of confidence and ability.

Reading dialogue out loud is very useful when trying to assess whether or not it is realistic or stilted. This technique can also identify places where children are tempted to use blocks of speech to deliver the story, rather than describing what is happening.

Step 4: Pair work – dialogue practice

You might like to get pupils to complete this short exercise to help them become more confident with using dialogue. Ask your pupils, just for fun, to write their very own example of clunking, bad dialogue. The more unrealistic and leaden, the better. They could even develop dialogue for a well-known story such as *The Three Little Pigs* where the pig in the brick house might say:

> 'What is the matter you silly brother pigs? Where are your houses? Destroyed? You stupid pigs, you should have been clever like me and not made your house from straw or sticks. I cannot believe I am so very much cleverer than you two stupid ninnies. Hurry up brothers, and come to my house. It is built from brick and in a minute the Big Bad Wolf will be huffing and puffing outside but nothing will happen. I have built a big fire and when he comes down the chimney he will get burned.'

Pupils can take an extract from any such story and rewrite it in a similar way, as awful dialogue. A quality of very bad dialogue is that it tells the reader everything that happens, rather than showing the reader (this is another version of the 'show don't tell' rule). Readers like to discover the events of a story for themselves, working out what is happening, and wondering what is going to happen, as they turn the pages. If a reader is told the whole plot, in dialogue, then there is no incentive to read any further.

The 'bad dialogue' can be cast, and read out, and the very worst examples celebrated. If a child writes lucid, clear dialogue during this exercise they can be told to use the same standard and style in this *Persuasion: unexpected arrival* exercise.

Step 5: Review of the task before pupils start writing

Having done the preliminary work, children can be reminded of the exercise. Take time to go over the following guidance with them.

Guidance

- Follow the template. The whole exercise can take from two to three pages in length, depending upon the age of the pupil.
- Pupils are using this exercise just to write one episode or scene. It might make up a longer story later, or it could be used to create a short play.
- Children can start the work in class and take it home for completion at a later date. The exercise can also be drafted, then revised, over two separate class meetings.
- For the first time in this sequence of exercises, *dialogue is allowed.*

Start writing!

You may find it helpful to post the following questions up on the IWB in case anyone gets stuck or needs some help.

Questions to help your writing

1   Give the characters some activity – now that they can talk, avoid having them do something a bit more interesting than just standing around talking. The scene can become funny, or more dramatic, if the activity that your main character is engaged with tells us something about how much they want to get rid of the unexpected arrival. Give some thought as to where the scene takes place.
    For example:
  - The girl caught wearing her sister's favourite outfit could be trying to hide the clothes under the bed while she is trying to talk her sister into leaving her room.
  - The boy who wants to get Aunty Joyce not to join in his party might be decorating a cake, while he is trying to persuade his aunt that the party will be boring.

2   Now that you are finally allowed to use dialogue, it is important to remember the non-talking exercises – *atmosphere, props and place are important*. Most of your story will be told through the non-dialogue elements of your story and you must try to avoid having the characters tell us the story.

3   How are you going to set up the main character's problems right at the start? You only have one scene to do this in. What props, actions or other clues can you come up with to show who this person is and how they get on with those around them, without relying totally on dialogue, or what the person says?

4   To help you make your dialogue tight and well written, pupils might try this exercise. Every time anyone says something in a story, it is for a purpose. In stories and plays, dialogue is always there for a reason: to attack, persuade, buy time, evade, please.

Can you cut each line of conversation or dialogue to the one-word verb underlying it (for example, attack, deflect, persuade, seduce)?

This may not happen when you first write the scene down on the page, but look at your first draft and see if you can do it. If there are no underlying verbs (other than explaining, which is too emotionally neutral), is there enough conflict in the scene?

5   Remember the earlier exercises:

Where are your characters? What is the atmosphere? Can we tell anything about them from what they own, wear, or are decorated with? You can use ideas that you developed in the *Building atmosphere, Sharing a room, The character in the environment* and *Getting ready for a date* exercises in this work.

Are there any opportunities for planting any object, and having a pay-off?

Step 6: Giving feedback

Feedback should follow guidelines laid out in Chapter 4.5. As pupils read each other's work they can be reminded to ask themselves the following questions.

Feedback reminder

You should understand, as you read the work of other pupils:

- Who is the main character?
- Who are they expecting to arrive?
- Why do they want to get rid of their unwelcome guest so very badly?
- What happened in the end – did our hero get rid of this unwanted guest in time?

Summary

Through this exercise pupils learn to distinguish better between the differing functions of parts of speech and their appropriate usage. This exercise supports and develops writing in other areas of the curriculum. As pupils see that the correct use of dialogue and description is essential in a good story, this provides a strong incentive to employ techniques elsewhere. Pupils can better grasp the need for a polished writing style when they are rewarded with positive feedback from peers about their own creative work.

The use of dialogue will add a new dynamic to the feedback sessions, as pupils will receive much more immediate and appreciative responses to their writing, if work can be 'cast' and read out loud. The very immediacy of the feedback generated can be incredibly encouraging and even the weaker pieces of writing can be enlivened and their authors inspired and encouraged. When a piece of work is read out loud, and different characters' speech is read by different pupils, the author of the piece can 'hear' their own creation for the first time.

Pupils will be able to build upon and extend learning in earlier classes. As pupils work through these exercises you can reference previous exercises and remind children to use tools mastered in previous weeks. For example, as pupils work on *Persuasion: unexpected arrival* you can remind them that the weather outside the scene can play a part; that the characters in the scene might be more interesting if we can tell from the things they have around them, what kind of people they are. It is important to keep pupils on task and writing but if there is a moment when reference can be made to the previous week's work then this would be a useful moment to reinforce the value of each piece of student work.

In fact each of these exercises will be sharpening the pupils' range and ability and provides them with a toolkit that they can use to enrich their writing. As work is read out the teacher can reinforce earlier lessons, giving praise, for example:

- When a sudden, torrential storm interrupts a girl preparing to go to a party wearing her sister's favourite outfit (a tool learned in 4.1 *Building atmosphere* exercise).
- When we notice a giant, expensive gold ring in a box on the bedside table of the girl who is trying to get her younger sister to leave her alone to meet her boyfriend (a tool learned in 4.3 *Getting ready for a date* exercise).
- When we notice that Aunty Joyce has brought a big case of sheet music for parties with her, and an audition call for *The X Factor* (as learned in 4.2 *Sharing a room* and 4.3 *Getting ready for a date* exercises).

5.3   The awkward situation

Introduction

The awkward situation focuses on the development of a story in which the drama depends on either the refusal of one character to cooperate with the main character's plans, or where the environment itself is the obstacle. It also reinforces elements of storytelling covered in Chapter 4 including the importance of character, the use of 'planting and pay-off', together with story structure.

It introduces pupils to the following concepts:

- Drama of a story can be developed around an attempt by one character to persuade another character to go along with their wishes.
- The drama and tension in a story depends upon obstacles that block the plans of the main character.

- Seduction and persuasion are elemental scenes in storytelling and mastery of their structure will ensure that stories are compelling.
- This writing tool is described as engaging the reader's 'hope versus fear'. If this is secured, readers will be hooked.

The exercise builds upon work covered in 5.1 *The object and the obstacle* and 5.2 *Persuasion: unexpected arrival* by reinforcing the fact that:

- Each pivotal moment should build from a previous one.
- The frustration of the hero's desires is a fundamental component of all good storytelling.

Exercise 5.3: The awkward situation

You are going to write a scene where someone (the seducer) is trying desperately to persuade the other person to do something or to get something from another person. They are going to use charm and persuasion.

It is not going to be easy. They cannot just say 'Give me this' and the answer is 'Yes'. Then you would not have any problems and that means no story.

Your characters can talk in this exercise.

You have two options to choose from:

- *Option A*: An awkward situation where the person being persuaded is willing but the circumstances are all wrong.
- *Option B*: An awkward situation where the circumstances are absolutely perfect but the person being persuaded is not willing, for example, the mood, time of day and the place are perfect but the person will not go along.

Step 1: Classroom discussion – examples from fiction

Take the time to lead a discussion about examples of stories and films that include one or more of the awkward situation scenarios. Your pupils can be encouraged to add to the following list.

Examples from fiction and film

- How does Harry Potter first express an interest in Ginny Weasley and why doesn't he take her to her first dance? Who does he take in the end and does he have a good time?
- In *Cinderella*, why do the Ugly Sisters want to marry Prince Charming? What are the obstacles in the way of this plan?
- Rumpelstiltskin wants to get something . . . why can't he get it? How does he get it in the end?
- The Gingerbread Man wants the fox to carry him over the river. Does this work?
- The wolf wants Little Red Riding Hood to believe that he is in fact her grandma. What happens?
- In *High School Musical*, Sharpay Evans does not want Gabriella Montez to join the musical – how does she try to persuade Gabriella to give up on her plan?
- *For older pupils:* in *How to Lose a Guy in 10 Days*, the girl is determined to make the boy dislike her. She puts a pink furry toilet cover in his loo and a collection of teddies on his bed. She brings a 'love fern' around to his flat and phones him in the middle of the night to tell him everything that she ate that day.

Can pupils come up with any other ways that might be used try to get rid of someone who had a crush upon them, who they did not like at all?

Step 2: Classroom discussion – the art of persuasion

Pupils are now able to use dialogue to help their characters try to achieve what they most desire, using techniques developed following 5.1 *The object and the obstacle*.

If this is the first time pupils are using dialogue, it would be useful to review the guidelines included in 5.2 *Persuasion: unexpected arrival*.

Ask your pupils:

- Have you ever used your charms to try to get a particular toy, game or bicycle for Christmas?

- How did you go about persuading your parents and relatives to give you what you wanted?
- Have you ever seen a parent get a large tray of biscuits or cakes out of the oven and tell you that you cannot eat them because they have to cool down first, or they are being saved for someone who is visiting the next day?
- Have you ever wanted to watch your absolute favourite TV show only to be told that one of your parents wants to watch the snooker/football/tennis final?
- Have you ever heard the ice-cream van tune and gone to a parent to ask for money?

For older pupils:

- Has your bigger brother/sister ever had someone round on a date and tried to get rid of you so that they can have a romantic evening?
- Have you ever had a crush on a boy/girl and tried to get them to go on a date with you, like to see a film, to the funfair, or to the end of year disco?
- Was it easy?
- What kind of things got in your way?

This exercise is entitled *The awkward situation* and younger pupils will happily write about a vast range of seductive tools they use to get their needs and desires met.

Older pupils may choose to write along romantic lines. They could choose to write about an older brother or sister, or even their own experiences of trying to be alone with a prospective girlfriend/boyfriend to watch a movie and a younger kid getting in the way. It could be a scene where someone is trying to get a first romantic tryst or kiss.

Scenarios should be age appropriate and pupils can talk directly with a teacher if they think the material that they want to cover is too overt.

Step 3: Pair work – getting what you want

Pupils should now be able to come up with examples of times that they have managed to get what they wanted, the various setbacks they encountered, and times when all their tactics failed, and they did not get what they wanted.

Once the pairs have had ten minutes' discussion time, the teacher can get the partner in each pair to share their best or worst example of persuasion, or can get the pupils to share in groups.

Note: children should have the right to come up with ideas and either keep them to themselves, write them down and show only the teacher, or share them only with their allocated partner. They should never be forced to share anything that they don't want to with the whole class.

Step 4: Class feedback and summary

On the IWB, a summary of tactics that can be used to persuade can be written up, reinforcing the pupils' ideas and embellishing them. The tactics might be categorized as 'reasoning', 'sneaky', 'physical actions, distractions and tricks', 'being devious', 'bluffing' and so on.

Start writing!

You may find it helpful to post the following questions up on the IWB in case anyone gets stuck or needs some help.

Questions to help your writing

1 Talking is allowed as you write up your scene. Be careful not to tell the whole story through conversation – you now have a rich toolkit that you can use to tell your story. See notes regarding the use of dialogue in 5.2 *Persuasion: unexpected arrival*. Remember the environment, the atmosphere, and all the other elements that were developed in Chapter 4, should now be incorporated to make your story work.

2 The awkward situation could include the following:
   • Mum has let the tray of biscuits get cool but, just as the child is about to eat them, the aunt with the big appetite arrives.

- Mum gets her money out for the ice cream van but then an uncle starts on about ice creams being junk food and a cause of obesity.
- There is a third person there, an old aunt or uncle, or an ex-husband or ex-wife.
- Or the place is wrong, for example, a big sister is trying to get her first kiss from a boy during a noisy football game.
- The big brother is trying to cuddle up to a girl and she starts squeezing her spots in the mirror!

Or whatever you can come up with to make things as awkward, funny or dramatic as possible.

3   If you choose the situation where the person being persuaded is not willing, this could include the following:
- Mum is on a diet and the biscuits get locked up in a high cupboard.
- The ice cream money gets shut away, in Dad's unbreakable piggy bank.
- The girl is desperate for a bikini Barbie but her mum wears a burqa.
- The boy has a big crush on a much taller girl who does not like him at all and wants to go to the school disco with his best friend.

Or whatever you can come up with to make things as awkward, funny or dramatic as possible.

Step 5: Giving feedback

Feedback should follow guidelines laid out in Chapter 4.5. As pupils read each other's work they can be reminded to ask themselves the following questions.

Feedback reminder

You should understand, as you read the work of other pupils:

- What the goal of the 'persuader' or 'seducer' is.
- What kind of resistance or problems are caused by either the environment/situation or by the person being seduced.

- What happened: did the seducer get what they wanted?
- Or not?
- Was there a twist?

Summary

Seduction and *persuasion* scenes are critical in storytelling. Readers should always be interested enough to *hope* that the main character will get what they want, and there should be sufficient obstacles to keep readers *afraid* that the whole project will not work.

To illustrate this point, the teacher can ask:

- Has anyone ever seen a bad film?
- Or given up on reading a story before the end?
- Or heard a boring speech?

Pupils may have examples of stories or texts where this happened. A list of pupils' suggestions can be created on the IWB. It is usually easy for pupils to describe bad movie plots. For example pupils can be asked why they were bored, and what they disliked about the various stories. Ultimately, the teacher will be able to summarize all the different reasons for these failures as being based upon a failure to engage the reader's or viewer's interest or engage their emotions.

This writing tool is described as engaging the reader's 'hope versus fear'. If this is not secured, readers will give up on your story after just a few lines. Examples of reader engagement are readily found in literature, proving that such scenes are a crucial building block for good fiction.

For example ask children to name their favourite books or movies and they should then be able to locate a scene within each that worked in the same way as the scene that they have just written.

Pupils at Key Stage 2 onwards have a growing awareness that those closest to them and those they depend upon for food, shelter and the meeting of their most immediate needs have sometimes very different wants, needs and desires from their own, and operate from a great range of motivations. They may have begun to work out why parents put a brake on fun, or they may resent it, but they should be able by now to examine the motivations behind the behaviour of others.

This exercise stretches and reinforces the pupils' development of a sophisticated range of social skills that they will need to operate successfully in a range of environments. Children may also now be aware that the adults in their lives are sometimes not totally consistent, emotionally, and can even be capricious, and that there may be differences of opinion between parents that can be exploited, and in such experiences lie tools that can be used to create really good fiction.

They may also be aware that skills of persuasion are actually a vital survival tool both in the pecking order of their own school playgrounds and in the world of work and outside endeavour that their parents occupy.

5.4 Making a bad situation worse

Introduction

Making a bad situation worse enables pupils to begin to develop the ability to use cleverly constructed, layered conflict to add drama to their writing. They may also begin to develop an element of conflict resolution from this exercise, and an understanding that their own experiences of difficulties can be used as inspiration for storytelling.

It introduces pupils to the following concepts:

- The drama of a story can be developed around one pivotal moment of confession, persuasion or introduction.
- Confession and meetings that go wrong are elemental scenes in storytelling and mastery of their structure will ensure that stories are compelling.

The exercise builds upon work covered in 5.1, 5.2 and 5.3 by reinforcing the following facts:

- Each pivotal moment should build from a previous one.
- The frustration of the hero's desires is a fundamental component of all good storytelling.

- This writing tool is described as engaging the reader's 'hope versus fear'. If this is secured, readers will be hooked.
- The drama and tension in a story depends upon obstacles that block the plans of the main character.

Note: this exercise is broken into three choices of subject matter, each with two options, with three sets of classroom prompts and points of discussion.

Exercise 5.4:   Making a bad situation worse

Choose from one of the *three* choices described:

1   Breaking the bad news
2   The confession
3   Boy meets a girl's father

Choice 1: Breaking the bad news

Option A for younger pupils: Excluded or expelled girl/boy

A pupil must tell his/her mother that they have been expelled/excluded from school, or that they have been caught stealing. The pupil goes to see their mother, at home or work (or some other place) but wherever it is, the mother is involved with a distraction or activity that makes it impossible for the woman to understand what her son/daughter is telling her.

Option B for older pupils: Pregnant girl

A young woman must tell her mother that she is pregnant. She goes to see her mother, at home or work (or some other place) but wherever it is, the mother is involved with a distraction or activity that makes it impossible for her to understand what her daughter is telling her.

Step 1: Pair work – the trouble

Your pupils need to decide what kind of trouble their character is in. Get them to talk about times when they have been in trouble with their parents, or they have done something that they know their parents will be really annoyed about.

- How have they delayed getting to the point and confessing?
- How did it go when they did confess?
- Pupils can choose a different kind of trouble that the girl or boy could be in, if they like. It just needs to be big, big trouble.

Step 2: Pair work – embarrassment

The girl/boy cannot just come straight out with the confession. They are too frightened. Now your pupils need to work out why their main character feels embarrassed about this confession. They are not going to get straight to the point. They might even tell a story about someone they know who is in trouble – anything to delay the evil moment when they must tell the truth.

If they have ever got into big trouble themselves their story could be about a child in a similar situation – and in this way the pupil can test out how the parent is going to react when they finally do confess.

- What kinds of tactics have they ever used, or imagined using, to break bad news to their parents?
- Did their fears, about how their parents would react, come true?
- How did they feel?
- How can you make the situation as bad as it could possibly be for this boy/girl?
- For example, if the child is confessing to being caught stealing, maybe the mother is a policewoman – giving a talk at a school, about the evils of stealing?
- Could religious, cultural or social beliefs make this scene more stressful?

The girl/boy needs to make attempts to tell the mother the bad news in a roundabout way – in writing, this is called *'indirection.'* It can be a very effective way of expressing the inner conflict of a character.

Think of what it would be like to be the young woman or child. Ask pupils to come up with some ideas for ways they might 'get around' to the topic that they feel awkward talking about?

For example, a girl or boy who has been expelled might try to get their mother

- to talk about reasons why studying at school is not important
- or to talk about problems the mother had at school
- or to confess that she nearly got kicked out of school once
- or to talk about naughty Uncle Eric, who really was expelled and then went on to do really, really well and earn much more money than poor Mum, who stuck it out at school.

A girl who is pregnant might

- talk about how gorgeous a neighbour's baby is
- or mention some lovely clothes she has seen for 'larger' women
- or get her mother to talk about how wonderful she felt when she was pregnant
- or ask her mother why she didn't have a baby when she was really young
- or even ask her mother if she would like to look after a baby again!

Step 3: Classroom discussion – distracted parents

Children also need to talk about times when they have tried – and failed – to get their parents' attention when they were in trouble. What kinds of activities really distract parents?

These might include:

- The mother is busy on the phone planning a fabulously expensive birthday party to reward the daughter/son for being such a wonderful, good child and excellent pupil.
- The mother works as a judge and is in the middle of a big trial; she is very angry with people who leave school early or steal.

- The mother works in a hairdressing salon full of noisy hairdryers – she has a giant photo of her child on the wall of the salon to show off what a great child she has.
- The mother is in prison.
- The mother is moving out of the house to emigrate.
- The mother is trying to fix a car or a washing machine, shoe a horse or operate on a guinea pig etc.

The mother's distraction is crucial – remember, it would take a lot for a mother not to hear and understand that her son/daughter is in very deep trouble or that her daughter has been expelled from school or is pregnant.

Tip

If a child wishes, either of these confessions can be made to a father or other carer in the child's life.

The end of the scene is up to your pupils – the daughter/son does or does not get her mother to understand what kind of trouble they are in, or they fail, and the mother reacts, or doesn't.

The whole exercise can take from two to three pages in length, depending upon the age of the pupil.

Pupils are using this exercise just to write one episode or scene. It might make up a longer story later, or it could be used to create a short play.

Children can start the work in class and take it home for completion at a later date. The exercise can also be drafted, then revised, over two separate class meetings.

Dialogue is allowed.

Exercise 5.4: Making a bad situation worse

Choice 2: The confession

Option A for younger pupils: Crush on a sister's boyfriend

A girl goes to her big sister to tell her that she has a big crush on her big sister's boyfriend. Figure out why it is important for the girl to make the confession at this particular time. Also, what setting and/or activity can you give the sister that would make it difficult for the girl to make this confession? (*Note:* feel free to experiment with gender . . . you could have a boy go to his older brother to talk about his crush upon his big brother's girlfriend)

Option B for older pupils: Having an affair

A woman goes to her sister to tell her that she is having an affair with her sister's husband. Figure out why it is important for the woman to make this confession at the particular time. Also, try to think about a situation or activity that the married sister could be engaged with that would make it difficult for the woman to make this confession?

Step 1: Pair work – why confess right now?

Get your pupils to talk about reasons why the younger brother or sister must make this confession at this time.

- Has an engagement just been announced?
- Perhaps a baby is on the way?
- Maybe the younger brother/sister has decided that their feelings are returned and they can no longer keep their feelings secret?
- Perhaps the older sister/brother has been having an affair also, or is planning to leave?

Step 2: Pair work – distracting the brother/sister

Get your pupils to talk about any squabbles they have had with friends or brothers and sisters over boyfriends and girlfriends.

- Why is the big sister/brother so very distracted that they cannot hear the confession?
- What distraction would create the biggest impact?

- Imagine if the bigger brother is a professional boxer who is hammering away at a punching bag when the scrawny younger brother shows up to make his confession.
- Imagine if the bigger sister is flicking through a 'wedding magazine' and writing up a guest list when her little sister shows up with her confession.
- Or the big sister is choosing baby clothes (because she is pregnant with this boyfriend's baby)?

Step 3: Pair work – who are these people?

Your pupils need to work out who their characters are. Get them to share their ideas for this exercise.

- Who is the girl or boy? How old are they? What is their relationship with the person that they must make this confession to?
- What kind of job or profession does the brother/sister have? How does this occupation enter into the scene?
- Could religious, cultural or social beliefs make this scene more stressful? What if a girl is confessing to having fallen in love with the man that her older sister is having an arranged marriage with?
- If you have studied the story of Romeo and Juliet, you would know that sometimes family rivalry can cause problems in romance.

Exercise 5.4: Making a bad situation worse

Choice 3: Boy meets a girl's father

Option A for younger pupils: Meeting the girl's father

A boy is going to meet the father of the girl he has a big crush on for the first time. The young man is so nervous that, although he has taken care to dress up well, he falls into a big muddy ditch full of pig manure on the way to the house and has torn his clothes in a hedge. He is also very late.

Option B for older pupils: Meeting girlfriend's father

A young man is going to meet the father of the young woman he loves for the first time. The young man is so nervous that he gets a little drunk for the big event. What happens? Does he blow it? Does the father understand?

You don't need to show the boy getting drunk. Start with him tipsy already. Let us see the manifestation of this in the scene with the father, with props, situations and actions. The end of the scene is up to you – the young woman can come in at the end of the scene to resolve it or make things worse.

Step 1: Class discussion – examples

Take the time to lead a discussion about examples of stories and films that include one or more of the 'Meet the father' scenarios. Your pupils can be encouraged to add to the following examples.

Examples from fiction and film

- When Shrek first goes to Neverland he hopes to make a great impression on Fiona's father – can you remember why this goes wrong?
- In the film series of *Meet the Parents*, a young man must make a good impression on his future father-in-law, but everything goes very badly wrong. Can you remember why?

Step 2: Pair work – who are these people?

Get your pupils to talk about who their characters are:

- What does the father do for a living?
- What about the boy – has he just been expelled from school?

- Or the young man, has he just started out upon a career that will make him very successful?
- Or is he planning to work his way around the world with a begging bowl?

The greater the difference between the father and the boy or young man – in terms of their approaches to money and dating – the greater the drama. What happens? Does he blow it? Does the father understand? You don't need to show the boy getting into all the trouble on the way. Start with him filthy, dirty, torn and tattered already. Let us see the manifestation of this in the scene with the father, with props, situations and actions. The end of the scene is up to you – the girl can come in at the end of the scene to resolve it or make things worse.

Step 3: Pair work – distractions and misunderstandings

The boy's goal, as he likes the daughter a lot, would be to make a good impression upon her father. Can you think up lots of things that are going to prevent the boy from achieving his goal? Remember to use tools learned in the earlier exercises, and think about where this meeting takes place.

Give the characters some activity – do not just have them standing around talking. Give them something to do, and give some thought as to where the scene takes place.

- What if Dad is cleaning up all the droppings in the Elephant House, when the young man arrives, and Dad gets the young man to help him clean up?
- What if the young man arrives in a fancy fast car and Dad drives a pony and cart, because he believes that driving cars will destroy the planet?
- What if Dad is busy skinning and chopping up a deer that he has shot, that he wants to serve for dinner. He tries to get the young man to help cut up the carcass, but the young man is a vegetarian?
- What if the young man brings some juicy steaks with him and Dad is on a wheat-grass fast and has not eaten meat for 20 years?

- What if Dad is busy changing the nappy of the girl's new baby brother, and the Dad starts telling the young boy how he hopes that his daughter will be able to get pregnant and have a baby very soon, because babies are the best thing in life?

Start writing!

You may find it helpful to post the following questions up on the IWB in case anyone gets stuck or needs some help.

Questions to help your writing

Before you write any of the exercises, you should *know your characters.*

1   In *Breaking the bad news* – who is the girl or boy? How old? What is the relationship with the mother, what is her profession, and does that enter into the scene?
2   In *The confession* – what is the relationship with the sister, or brother, who has to listen to this confession? Close? Distant? Were they rivals growing up, or close confidants?
3   In *Boy meets a girl's father* – who is the boy? Why does he love this girl? Who is the father? What is his profession and how can that be used to intensify the conflicts, obstacles in the scene?

Talking is allowed as you write up your scene. Be careful not to tell the whole story through conversation – you now have a rich toolkit that you can use to tell your story. See notes regarding the use of dialogue in 5.2 *Persuasion: unexpected arrival.*

Remember that the environment, the atmosphere, and all the other elements that were developed in Chapter 4, should now be incorporated to make your story work.

How are you going to set up the main character's problems right at the start? You only have one scene to do this in. What props, actions or other clues can you come up with to show who this person is and how they get on with those around them, without relying totally on dialogue, or what the person says?

Who is the most important person in the story at that moment? The person with the greatest desire will dominate a scene. Thus in the *Harry Potter* books, when Voldemort appears and tries to defeat Harry, his evil desire dominates the story. When the wolf is dressed as grandma and tries to convince the girl that he is her grandma, his desire for a tasty snack dominates the story at that moment. If you know which character is dominating the scene, it will help you to write it.

To help you make your dialogue tight and well written, can you reduce each line of conversation or dialogue to the one-word verb underlying it (for example, attack, deflect, persuade, seduce)? This may not happen when you first pour the scene down on the page, but look at your first draft and see if you can do it. If there are no underlying verbs (other than explaining, which is too emotionally neutral), is there enough conflict in the scene?

Are there any opportunities for planting any object, and having a pay-off?

Step 4: Giving feedback

Feedback should follow guidelines laid out in Chapter 4.5. As pupils read each other's work they can be reminded to ask themselves the following questions.

Feedback reminder

You should understand, as you read the work of other pupils:

- Who is the main character?
- What kind of resistance or problems are caused by either the environment/situation or by the person they are either making a confession to or trying to make a good impression upon?
- What happened after the confession or the meeting with the father? Did the main character achieve what they wanted? That is: make a great impression on the father or get away

> with their confession and have the news accepted without any repercussions?
> - Or not?
> - Was there a twist?

Summary

One of our favourite techniques to kick start discussion before this exercise is to ask pupils: 'Hands up anyone who always gets on with every single member of their families?' Of course, no hands go up!

Through this exercise the children can begin to understand their own personal stories of family conflict within the wider context of universal human conflict. Facing up to awkward situations and dealing with difficult truths or confessions are essential tools for the social and psychological survival of children as they move into early adolescence.

Children also can begin to develop the ability to use cleverly constructed, layered conflict to add drama to their writing. They may also begin to develop not only for their stories, but also for themselves, an element of conflict resolution from this exercise.

This exercise may also provide a forum in which they can test out happy endings to their own difficult situations. As the pair work involves an element of role-playing, pupils can potentially use the exercise to work out how problems in their own lives could be worked out. The exercise will also help to build group cohesion and empathy.

Furthermore children can have the stories of their own lives validated and they can begin to understand that the most awful or awkward situations that they face can have a great value – the experiences can become material for fiction, but, most importantly, pupils will discover that they have the power to change the ending of any story within their own lives.

A useful example of the transformative possibilities of life experiences can be seen in the work of J.M. Barrie, the author of *Peter Pan*. He was deeply affected when he was a child by the death of an older brother, and in the story of Peter Pan he created a young boy, full of life, fun and adventure, who gets to live forever.

J.K. Rowling has talked openly about having no present contact with her father, with whom she had a very difficult relationship – yet the *Harry*

Potter books are full of wonderful father figures, and Harry is ultimately protected from the very evil figure of Voldemort by the incredible power of his parents' love and support for him.

Charles Dickens' own father was sent to a debtor's prison, and at age 12 Charles had to work in a shoe polish factory. His novels contain many sympathetic stories of children who triumph over terrible life experiences.

Teachers may be able to add other examples, or get pupils to add to the list of authors who are known to have used the fabric of their own lives, particularly painful elements, to create great fiction. There are many more examples where writers have used experiences in their own lives as an inspiration for great stories. A good writer can transform imperfect or difficult elements of their own lives into the fabric of their own writing, and of course, once transformed into fiction, the endings can be changed. This is one of the greatest joys of writing, and one that pupils can gain an insight into through this exercise.

6

Planting and pay-off

Introduction

Chapters 6, 7 and 8 enable children to build upon fundamental skills developed through the earlier chapters. It is possible to use the templates within these chapters as stand-alone writing exercises, but it is assumed that children at this stage will have fairly well-developed writing skills, including the ability to create strong characters, obstacles and the ability to employ atmosphere and environment effectively. Reference to earlier exercises that can enrich work for the later chapters is made where relevant. The layout of Chapters 6, 7 and 8 is simpler, because it is assumed that pupils will not need to be helped to develop fundamental story components before moving on to develop the entire narrative.

In this chapter we present three story templates:

- 6.1 *The love story*
- 6.2 *The misunderstanding*
- 6.3 *The caper.*

These three themes underpin many favourite children's stories.

Working with these themes, using the templates, builds confidence, particularly among children who do not yet have a love of reading but perhaps who, for a variety of reasons, have spent many hours watching television and films. Their familiarity with a range of genres and plots will empower such children – who might feel disenfranchised when more literary texts are discussed – to make a significant contribution to class work.

If pupils have difficulty thinking of archetypal characters who might fit within the following templates, at this stage it is recommended that they complete the 8.1 *Character profiles* exercise. Your pupils will then have a rich cast of characters that can be used in a range of story templates.

The templates are designed to generate outlines that can be used to create completed, longer fiction. Creating an outline provides pupils with a solid understanding of the way such templates work. This reinforces the theory that underpins the approach to writing embedded within this book: that writing is a craft that can be developed through practical exercises.

Outlining is a technique used by writers to hammer out the main beats of their stories before they have committed many hours to a text, and at a stage when major changes can still be made. At this stage, outlines are being used because the plots generated will be sufficient to support a complete story or even a novel or a film. Pupils can be asked to complete the stories based upon these templates in their own time, or class time can be set aside to enable pupils to write out the whole text.

Children will be able to take their understanding of the way these fundamental templates work to help with the development of their own fiction, and to assist with their understanding of texts as they become more sophisticated readers and viewers of texts.

6.1 The love story

Exercise 6.1: The love story

Write an outline for the story following the guidelines below.

An outline is a plan for a story, and just contains the basic plot that you want to write.

Scene 1

- Introduce us to a character that you think is the *least capable of love*. If this is difficult, please see 8.1 *Character profiles*.
- As they are busy trying to get on with their lives and keep to themselves, another character enters their life, and invades their precious isolation.

Scene 2

- The main character fights the realization that they are becoming dependent on or in love with the new arrival.
- They take active steps to avoid getting more involved.
- Despite this, they cannot get the newcomer to leave.

Scene 3

- All this is making life really difficult for your main character's attempts to be alone again.
- Finally they must do something really drastic to get to be alone again.

What happens?

Step 1: Classroom discussion – examples

First, to enable your pupils to deal successfully with this subject, you need to remind pupils that love does not have to be romantic love. Love is a central theme in many of the children's favourite stories and they should be familiar with the many different kinds of love through their own knowledge of contemporary narratives.

Pupils can contribute their ideas or a list of stories that they have come across where a character is determined to be alone, and to reject love and friendship, or to find it. Reference can be made to texts studied in class.

Examples from fiction and film

- Shrek just wants to be alone in his swamp at the beginning of his story.
- The grumpy old man in the film *Up* does not like the boy scout who visits him and wants to be left alone.
- In *Brother Bear*, the grumpy older bear does not want to be followed by the orphaned bear.

- In *Home Alone*, the boy wants a peaceful Christmas away from his noisy family.
- In *The Lion King*, Zimba thinks he has killed his father, and runs away to be alone. However, instead of solitude he makes friends with a warthog and a meerkat.
- In *Toy Story*, the cowboy wants Andy to play with him, to win Andy's love back again and not let Andy just play with Buzz Lightyear.
- The Seven Dwarfs, particularly Grumpy, do not want a girl, Snow White, to live with them.
- In *The Jungle Book*, the Black Panther, Baghera, does not want to look after Mowgli at all.
- In the *High School Musical* series, the friends learn that they must all work together, and develop affection and respect for each other, to create something worthwhile.
- In the *Harry Potter* books, victory over Voldemort ultimately depends upon the love and support of Harry's group of friends and teachers at Hogwarts, and upon the love of his parents.
- The dogcatcher in *Santa Buddies* hates dogs and wants to be alone; but he does not succeed.
- In *How to Lose a Guy in 10 Days*, the heroine wants to make the hero run away from her, not fall in love with her.

Children will have seen situations involving characters like these in many books and films. It is worth noting that the character that wants to be alone often learns, during the course of their adventures, that being alone is not the best way to live. Thus Shrek returns to his swamp having learned that he needs Donkey in his life, and happily in love with the ogress, Fiona.

If children have seen any classic romantic films designed for older audiences, they will have come across many examples of the romantic form of love. The template pupils are going to employ to write their outlines is used to provide structure to many, if not most, stories in which the ultimate goal is one of the many varieties of love.

In addition to children's knowledge of existing texts, those who have completed earlier exercises will have created stories based upon a character's love, devotion and affection for things, hobbies, people or animals.

- In 4.1 *Building atmosphere*, maybe there was a character that was in love with their teddy bear?
- In 4.2 *Sharing a room*, maybe someone wrote about a character devoted to a particular sport, hobby, or movie star?
- In 4.4 *The character in the environment*, maybe pupils wrote about a character's adoration and affection for their ballet or soccer teacher, for a pet, a home, a place, some kind of trainer or inspirational person?
- In 5.3 *The awkward situation*, perhaps pupils wrote about someone who was trying their best to escape from the possibility of love?

Step 2: Pair work – who is this person?

In pairs or small groups, pupils can talk about characters that they consider to be the least capable of love. They could have written about such a character if they have completed the 8.1 *Character profiles* exercise. If pupils have copies of this character profile, it might be worth sharing a selection with the whole class at this point.

Think about why someone would want so very desperately to be alone:

- What experiences have they had that could have made them feel this way?
- Why would someone try so very desperately to get rid of another person who threatened their solitude by offering them kindness and companionship?

Step 3: Pair work – the unwanted intruder

Remember: you are going to describe a main character who wants to be alone, a second character who arrives and is going to try to destroy your main character's precious isolation?

The new character must have something special to offer that threatens to break down your main character – the protagonist's – defences. Pupils can work out what kind of character might pose a big enough threat to their main character's determination to be alone.

They can work from the list discussed earlier: Donkey (*Shrek*), the warthog (*The Lion King*), Buzz Lightyear (*Toy Story*) and the Seven Dwarfs (*Snow White*) are all very strong characters with particular qualities.

The second character is going to struggle to stay with the main character for their very own, unique reasons, hanging on despite all the rejection from your main character. Pupils need to work out why anyone would stick it out in such a situation.

Examples from fiction and film

- It might be out of a sense of duty. Remember Mowgli, in *The Jungle Book*, who almost gets eaten by a snake when he is abandoned? Baghera does not want to look after Mowgli but he cannot leave him to be eaten by a snake or a tiger.
- They are stubborn, or just have nowhere else to go (remember Donkey in *Shrek*).
- Or the new character might be classmates with your main character, or they might be co-workers on a job, or they might have to complete some task they have been given (*Brother Bear*).
- They are not very bright (the warthog in *The Lion King* is not portrayed as being very clever).

Whatever you come up with, it will have to be a strong enough motivation to keep your second character hanging on when the door is effectively slammed in their face, over and over again.

Step 4: Review of the task before pupils start writing

Having done the preliminary work, children can be reminded of the exercise. Take time to go over the following guidance with them.

Guidance

- Write a one and a half page outline for a story following the template set out at the beginning of this section. An outline is a plan for a story, and just contains the basic plot that you want to write.

- Details such as conversations or intricate detail about the environment are not important at this stage. The object of a story outline is to give us an idea of the overall shape of the story in broad brushstrokes.
- At this stage it is possible, and much simpler, to change basic parts of the plot around to make the story work. Once the outline is written, other pupils can provide feedback as to how to make your story work better, before you have taken the trouble to write the whole story.
- Each section of the outline should just be about a paragraph long.

Scene 1

- Introduce us to a character that you think is the *least capable of love*.
- As they are busy trying to get on with their lives and keep to themselves, another character enters their life, and interrupts their precious isolation.
- The new character must have something special to offer that threatens to break down your main character's defences.

Scene 2

- The main character fights the realization that they are becoming deeply attached to, dependent on or in love with the new arrival.
- They take active steps to avoid making a real friend, or getting more involved – perhaps trying to avoid the person, or attempting to drive them away, or whatever steps they can come up with.
- The other character continues to pursue, for whatever reason, and so hampers the main character's efforts to get rid of them. Love and friendship are not always reciprocal.
- Try to make it as difficult as you can for your main character to get what they want – throw as many obstacles at them as you can think of. Keep your readers hoping – or fearing – that your main character will get to be totally alone again.

- The second character might have their own, unique reasons, for hanging on despite all the rejection.

Scene 3

- All this gets in the way of your main character's attempts to be alone again, or avoid contact with others. You need to make it really difficult for your main character to get what they want.
- Finally they realize that they must do something really drastic to get to be alone again.
- The main character does something very drastic to restore their precious isolation.
- What happens? Is your main character going to be able to adapt to the change, or do they return to living alone, without affection, love or company, happy or unhappy to be alone again?

Start writing!

Pupils should be given time to complete the exercise and then share their work and provide feedback.

You may find it helpful to post the following questions up on the IWB in case anyone gets stuck or needs some help.

Questions to help your writing

Remember the descriptive tools acquired during the exercises in Chapters 4 and 5, in particular the following:

- *Character work*: Who are these two people? How old are they? What do they look like? Why does the main character want to be alone? (This was covered in detail in Sections 4.1, 4.2, 4.3, 4.4 and 4.5.)
- *Environmental work*: Where is the story set? How does the environment affect events? (This was covered in detail in Sections 4.1, 4.2 and 4.3.)

- *Plot work*: Can you add any twists and turns, or make the situation even more difficult for your main character? (This was covered in detail in Sections 5.1, 5.2, 5.3 and 5.4.)
- *Economy of writing*: Remember to be selective with descriptions – pick the objects that define character. (This was covered in Chapter 4.)
- *Plant and pay-off*: Can you plant any objects in the first scene, when the main character is living happily alone, that can be used in later scenes? (This was covered in Chapter 4.)

Step 5: Giving feedback

Feedback should follow guidelines laid out in 4.5 *Giving feedback*. As pupils read each other's work they can be reminded to ask themselves the following questions:

Feedback reminder

As pupils read each other's work, they could use this list as a prompt to make sure that they understand the story. We should know from the outline:

- Who these people are.
- What the main character's life was like before the second character arrived.
- What the main character did to get rid of the second character.
- Whether or not they succeeded in getting to be alone again.
- How the second character felt about this.
- How the main character was affected by the events of the story: were they happy to be alone again, or happy to have their solitude restored, or sad that they 'won' and not happy to be alone any more?

It is sometimes useful with larger classes to get groups to choose their favourite example of the exercise to share with the whole class.

Summary

This exercise gives pupils the chance to revise the plot of the story before they become too committed to the structure, which can happen when the story is written out in too much detail. Although younger pupils may be very resistant to the idea of writing about 'love', the framework of the exercise should enable them to see that love is not limited to purely romantic love but that it is an elemental catalyst, and goal, in many of their favourite stories and films.

Through this exercise pupils build confidence in their ability to give and receive feedback and share ideas that can positively influence the development of a story on a very fundamental level. This is because feedback is being given at the outline stage, when it is still very easy to make changes.

Throughout the development of their craft as writers, your pupils will have been learning to come up with suggestions as to how the writing of other pupils can be improved, and incorporating or rejecting similar feedback on their own work. This process will enable pupils to realize that even their best loved stories may have undergone very many revisions before they were published. For young writers to get better, they must digest this most elemental skill: to revise, redraft, and polish. They may incorporate ideas shared by those kind enough to critique their work.

Through making changes at the outline stage, pupils are beginning to utilize the imaginations and ideas of others. Once the story outline has been drafted and written, pupils may want to write out the whole story. This can take place in their own time, as work taken home, or in class time if teachers want to devote more time to the exercise. Pupils can also develop a portfolio of outlines and then select the one that they enjoy the most, and that they get the most positive feedback upon, for development into a longer story.

6.2 The misunderstanding

Exercise 6.2: The misunderstanding

Write a one-page outline of a story following this basic pattern (each scene should be a paragraph or two long).

Details such as imagery and dialogue are not important at this stage. The idea is just to create a rough outline in broad brushstrokes.

Scene 1

- Introduce us to your main character (the protagonist) in the normal course of their life. They have a really big, obsessive ambition, dream or goal that rules their lives.
- While they are wrapped up in trying to achieve their dreams, some misunderstanding happens, that results in a major problem for your main character.
- Only we the readers (or audience) know about this misunderstanding. (For example, perhaps this person is mistaken for someone else, or mistakes somebody for someone else.)

Scene 2

- The main character tries to deal with this new problem, but as they do so, things just get worse, all because of the initial misunderstanding, which, again, no one but *the audience, or we the readers*, know about.
- At some stage during this second scene of the story, one or more characters may become aware of the initial misunderstanding.
- The problem is that this second character or characters, rather than reveal the truth, now uses it to their advantage. At last, the situation becomes totally desperate for the main character (protagonist), who must now take some drastic action.

Scene 3

- The truth about the initial misunderstanding becomes clear to all.

> • This is followed by the resolution. This is where, for the main character, life goes back to normal or it is changed forever by what has happened during your story.

Step 1: Classroom discussion – contexts

This exercise will make sense only if you develop a very strong character with a particular, unique and very obvious goal. You may have written about an ambitious character if you have already completed 8.1 *Character profiles*. Can you think of anyone you know, or have seen on TV or in film, who has a very strong ambition?

Some popular TV shows are devoted exclusively to people with big dreams – talent shows that try to find the next big star, like *The X Factor, Strictly Come Dancing*, *The Apprentice*, even the *Tracy Beaker* series.

Reality TV often focuses upon characters who are willing to make all kinds of sacrifices to achieve fame – eat revolting food, struggle to overcome obstacles, dive into icy pools, whatever the show's producers think will test them to their limits.

You may have noticed that, quite often, the dreams of the people auditioning for or taking part in reality shows are not matched by their talents or abilities.

Discussing these examples in class can help pupils gain a better understanding.

Examples from fiction and film

- In the *Just William* series, most of William's problems stem from ambitious plans to achieve things beyond his reach.
- In the *Charlie and Lola* books, Lola is often determined to launch plans that result, for many reasons, in failure.
- In *Tootsie*, the character played by Dustin Hoffman is a man who wants to get a good part in a soap opera; he disguises himself as a woman to get a part and this creates misunderstanding.

- In *Mr Big*, a child wants to become a man (but becomes a child inside a man's body).
- In *Mr Bean*, the main character wants to do simple things, like go on holiday, or enjoy a Christmas dinner, but he is so eccentric that we know things will not go smoothly.
- Captain Jack Sparrow in *Pirates of the Caribbean* never quite succeeds in his goals; something always seems to get in his way.

Children can add to this a list of ambitious historical figures who struggled to achieve a more lasting goal: Scott of the Antarctic, William the Conqueror, Adolf Hitler, Queen Boudicca, Winston Churchill, Aung San Suu Kyi, Mahatma Gandhi, Nelson Mandela, Florence Nightingale, Queen Elizabeth I, Margaret Thatcher, or favourite performers, cricketers, footballers or tennis players.

These are all people who have overcome or are struggling against incredible odds to achieve their dreams. If you have done some work on the Paralympics or Olympics you will have learned the stories of people who fight to achieve great things. Even your own parents, family members and relatives may have worked with determination to help you, or to get you the things that you wanted.

There are also characters who fight – sometimes heroically – and can never achieve their dreams. Can you think of any people like this?

The soldiers who fought in the First World War, or on losing sides in the Second World War, and those fighting on both sides in present-day conflicts have also fought with great determination and perhaps ambition.

We remember mountain climbers and adventurers who did not succeed in their goals as much as we celebrate the achievements of those who did.

There are also comic characters that we love because we know that they will *never* succeed in their goals. The structure and set-up of a comedy depends upon a character who can never really succeed and who will never learn from their mistakes.

Think of cartoon characters in particular and other individuals:

- The Coyote will never catch the Road Runner.
- Tom will never eat Jerry.
- The Wicked Wolf, no matter which children's story he appears in, never seems to get a good dinner.

- Basil Fawlty, who ran a terrible hotel called *Fawlty Towers*, never succeeded in his ambition to run the best hotel ever.
- Mr Bean has lots of dreams and desires that never seem to come true in the way that he wants.

Pupils can make some notes of ideas that they have developed for their own, very ambitious characters.

Step 2: Pair work – obstacles

Once pupils have a clear idea of a very ambitious character, they should now spend some time thinking about how to give their character big problems and obstacles that look set to destroy their dreams.

The exercise asks pupils to think up some kind of misunderstanding that is really going to block their characters from achieving their dreams. Pupils can discuss, in pairs, the kind of misunderstanding that could work in their story. The misunderstanding could arise from something that your character has kept secret, or hidden, or some lie that they have told in the past, or a character flaw that has been revealed.

If you have a strong character, with a very definite ambition, that will be very difficult to achieve, you are almost ready to start writing. Can you come up with any twists?

Step 3: Classroom discussion – bad stories

What makes a bad story?

You can ask pupils to give you the names of stories and films that they did not enjoy. Note each name on a board, and ask them for a few details as to why they did not like the text. Once you have excluded texts rejected on the basis of personal taste (the pupils concerned admit that they hate romances, vampire stories, or action stories and so on), the reasons for rejecting the story can probably be summed up by the following:

- They did not care what happened.
- They were not interested in whether or not the character succeeded.
- They could not concentrate on the story and started thinking about something else.
- They could not follow the story.

The average Hollywood feature film costs over $50 million and takes over five years of hard work by teams of different professionals, working full-time.

Novelists struggle for years to draft and redraft their stories, then may have to send their completed work out to many agents to find someone willing to publish their book. If, at the end of all this time, audiences and readers 'do not care', put the book down, or want to walk out of the film, then all that effort and money has been wasted.

The solution, to engage your readers or audience, and to stop them feeling bored or distracted, is to base their narrative upon a really *strong, engaging character*. A strong character does not have to be a perfect person. In fact, perfection will get in the way of readers or viewers being made to care about your character.

Step 4: Classroom discussion – good stories

Next you can ask pupils to give you the names of stories and films that they really love and would be happy to recommend to others. One example per pupil should be enough. Note each name on a board, and ask pupils for a few details as to why they enjoyed the book or film.

The reasons can be summed up by the following:

- They really cared what happened.
- They were really interested in whether or not the character succeeded.
- They could only follow the story – they went to their rooms and could not stop reading for hours, or they watched the movie and forgot everything until the lights went up at the end.
- The story was clear and easy to follow.

At this stage in the course, pupils should have a strong idea, themselves, through the giving and receiving of feedback, as to the qualities of a good story.

The list generated on the board can also be used now to create a list of the characteristics of the pupils' fictional heroes and heroines.

These might include:

- People who we can identify with, because they have weaknesses, or they have difficult family or relationship problems that are similar to our own.
- People who are flawed.
- Those who struggle against insurmountable odds.
- Characters that are multidimensional, who have fully rounded lives, families and friends.
- Characters that we can understand and who we know something interesting and unique about ... their hobbies, likes, dislikes, relationships and so on.

Pupils now need to put their ambitious character into the template and create a story around them.

Start writing!

You may find it helpful to post the following questions up on the IWB in case anyone gets stuck or needs some help.

Questions to help your writing

Remember the descriptive tools acquired during the exercises in Chapters 4 and 5, in particular the following:

1. *Character work*: Who are the characters? How old are they? What do they look like? Why does the main character want to achieve their ambition?
2. *Environmental work*: Where is the story set? How does the environment affect events?
3. *Plot work*: Can you add any twists and turns, or make the situation even more difficult for your main character?
4. *Economy of writing*: Remember to be selective with descriptions – pick the objects that define character.
5. *Plant and pay-off*: Can you plant any objects in the first scene, when the main character is living happily alone, that can be used in later scenes?

Step 5: Giving feedback

Feedback should follow guidelines laid out in Chapter 4.5. As pupils read each other's work they can be reminded to ask themselves the following questions:

Feedback reminder

As pupils read each other's work, they could use this list as a prompt to make sure that they understand the story. We should know from the outline:

- Who the main character is.
- What was the main character's life like at the start of the story?
- How the misunderstanding came about.
- Whether or not the main character succeeded in overcoming the obstacles created by the misunderstanding.
- How the other characters in the story felt about this.
- How the main character was affected by the events of the story: were they happy to achieve their goals, or did they find out that success did not make them happy?
- Were they upset not to achieve their goals, or pleased because they realized that their big ambition was not worthwhile?

Summary

Through this exercise, pupils can learn to access stories from history and other subject areas, including sport, science and the arts. They can create stories based upon favourite sporting or historical characters. Above all, this exercise helps pupils understand that *character is story*. The key to this exercise is the creation of a very strong character with a clear goal. Once that is done, the story and situation will be generated from the character.

Pupils have also gained experience of working with one of the most fundamental story templates. They can bring this experience to deconstruct the work of other authors.

6.3 The caper

Exercise 6.3: The caper

Scene 1

- Introduce us to a character in their usual routine.
- Early in the story, this character gets an idea to perform a caper.
- Show us how they got the idea.

Scene 2

- The main character plans and gets ready.
- They must overcome obstacles and problems as they get all the things they need ready for the caper.
- Finally everything is in place, the preparations are complete, and the caper is set to be launched.

Scene 3

- The main character carries out their plan.
- Does it succeed or not?
- Is there a twist, or an unexpected occurrence? What happens at the end?

Step 1: Class discussion – examples

This kind of story or scene within a story involves a lead character assembling a group to perform some kind of prank. This story will have three main scenes. Your pupils should be able to contribute to the following list of examples that employ the caper template, and are used in their favourite stories.

Examples from fiction and film

All these narratives involve scenes during which characters must make a plan, collect weapons or equipment, then launch an adventure:

- *Prince Caspian*
- *The Lion, the Witch and Wardrobe*
- *Peter Pan*
- *The Hobbit*
- *The Lord of the Rings*
- *The Famous Five* series
- *Harry Potter*
- *The Secret Seven* series
- *Just William*

Examples from film:

- *Star Wars*
- *Indiana Jones*
- *The Lavender Hill Mob*
- *Oceans Eleven*
- *The James Bond* series
- *Lara Croft Tomb Raider* (movie)

Step 2: Class discussion – obstacles

Children can discuss examples taken from the list, where the best laid plans of a gang of friends always encounter great obstacles.

For example:

- In *The Lion, the Witch and Wardrobe*, the death of Aslan makes the quest, to rid Narnia of the White Witch, seem doomed.
- In *Peter Pan*, when Captain Hook finally gets to have a sword fight with Peter, all seems lost.
- In *The Lord of the Rings*, the gang is slowly reduced to just two characters, Frodo and Sam, and at the very moment when it seems they will achieve their goal, Frodo is too weak to throw the ring away and all seems lost.

Encourage the children to add to this list.

Step 3: Pair work – developing characters

In pairs or small groups, pupils can talk about characters that they consider would work well in a caper.

This could be a choice from their 8.1 *Character profiles* exercise, for example, the 'Most ambitious person', or another that they think might suit the story.

Step 4: Review of the task before pupils start writing

Having done the preliminary work, children can be reminded of the exercise. Take time to go over the following guidance with them.

Guidance

- Write a one and a half page outline for a story following the basic pattern described. An outline is a plan for a story, and just contains the basic plot that you want to write.
- Details such as conversations or settings are not important at this stage. The object of a story outline is to give us an idea of the overall shape of the story in broad brushstrokes.
- At this stage it is possible, and much simpler, to change basic parts of the plot around to make the story work. Once the outline is written, other pupils can provide feedback as to how to make your story work better, before you have taken the trouble to write the whole story.
- Each section of the outline should just be about a paragraph long.

Scene 1

- Introduce us to a character in their usual routine.
- Early in the story, this character gets an idea to perform a caper.

When the story begins, is it in the middle of a normal day, or is the character under some other kind of pressure from a job, a problem at school, or at home, with parents or family, or other situation which might make

---

what starts happening to them as your story gets going, that much more difficult to deal with? How did they get the idea? Who gave it to them?

You should show us the generation of the idea, how it happens. Make it a memorable moment.

Scene 2

- The main character plans and gets ready.
- They must overcome obstacles and problems as they get all the things they need ready for the caper.
- Finally everything is in place, the preparations are complete, and the caper is set to be launched.

Tell us the details, have the character gather props or put together a gang of helpers if this is needed.

Perhaps they will have to rehearse the caper? In which case consider making us aware of things that might go wrong, or that must go right, when the real caper begins.

Scene 3

- The main character carries out their plan.
- Does it succeed or not?
- Is there a twist, or an unexpected occurrence? What happens at the end?

Your main challenge will be in keeping readers worried about whether or not the plans will succeed all the way through the story.

Try to think of ways that you can raise your readers' hopes and fears about whether or not your hero will be able to get the caper ready.

What is at stake for your character? What will happen if they fail, or if someone discovers the caper before it is launched?

Start writing!

Pupils should be given time to complete the exercise and then share their work and provide feedback.

You may find it helpful to post the following questions up on the IWB in case anyone gets stuck or needs some help.

Questions to help your writing

At this stage children should be able to employ the descriptive tools acquired during the exercises in Chapters 4 and 5, in particular the following:

1   *Character work*: Who are the characters? How old are they? What do they look like? Why does the main character want to achieve their ambition?
2   *Environmental work*: Where is the story set? How does the environment affect events?
3   *Plot work*: Can you add any twists and turns, or make the situation even more difficult for your main character?
4   *Economy of writing*: Remember to be selective with descriptions – pick the objects that define character.
5   *Plant and pay-off*: Can you plant any objects in the first scene, when the main character is living happily alone, that can be used in later scenes?

Step 5: Giving feedback

Feedback should follow guidelines laid out in Chapter 4.5. As pupils read each other's work they can be reminded to ask themselves the following questions.

Feedback reminder

As pupils write, and later read each other's work, they could use this list as a prompt to make sure that they understand the story. We should know from the outline:

• Who is the main character and who are the main characters in the group of friends?

- What were the characters' lives like at the start of the story?
- How did the caper or adventure come about?
- Did the gang succeed in overcoming the obstacles they ran into?
- How did their opponents react?
- How were the characters affected by the events of the story: were they happy to achieve their goals, or did they find out that success did not make them happy? Were they upset not to achieve their goals, or pleased because they realized that their caper was not worthwhile?

Summary

This exercise gives pupils the chance to revise the plot of the story before they become too committed to the structure, which happens when the story is written out in great detail. In addition pupils build confidence in their ability to give and receive feedback and share ideas, as during the pair and group work they are able to see their contributions positively affecting the work of others.

As mentioned previously, even professional writers describe writing as rewriting. This means that the final version of a story may be nothing at all like the first draft or rough idea for that story.

Once their story outline has been drafted and written, pupils may want to write out the whole story. This can take place in their own time, as work taken home, or in class time if teachers want to devote more time to the exercise. Pupils can develop a portfolio of outlines and then select the one that they enjoy the most, and that they get the most positive feedback on, for development into a longer story.

This exercise equips children with an understanding of one of the most fundamental of story templates. Having completed this exercise they will be able to bring an awareness of this structure to future reading and viewing of texts.

CHAPTER 7

Twists and turns

Introduction

Chapters 6, 7 and 8 enable children to build upon fundamental skills developed through the earlier chapters. It is possible to use the templates within these chapters as stand-alone writing exercises, but it is assumed that children at this stage will have fairly well-developed writing skills, including the ability to create strong characters and obstacles and the ability to employ atmosphere and environment effectively. Reference to earlier exercises that can enrich work for the later chapters is cited where relevant. The layout of Chapters 6, 7 and 8 is simpler, because it is assumed that pupils will not need to be helped to develop fundamental story components before moving on to develop the entire narrative.

In Section 7.1 we present three story templates:

(a) *Revolt*
(b) *Revenge*
(c) *Escape*

Once again, these three themes underpin many of our favourite stories.

These templates are followed by exercises that are intended as a starting point for the more advanced exercises, from Section 7.2 onwards. These sections are:

- 7.2 *The world of the story*
- 7.3 *Story questions*
- 7.4 *Freytag's Triangle* (or classical three-act structure).

While not designed to generate a story on their own, the questions in this section can be used to develop and enrich any ideas that pupils come up with for writing of their own, independent of the scenarios in this book.

These prompts to narrative development should be saved, as answering the questions during the drafting stage will help pupils in all future creative and non-fiction writing.

7.1   Revolt, revenge, escape

Introduction

Choose one of the *three* options below. The whole exercise can take from two to ten pages in length, depending upon the age of the pupil.

Children can start the work in class and take it home for completion at a later date. The exercise can also be drafted, then revised, over two separate class meetings.

In this exercise children can use characters that they may have discussed and written about if they have done the 8.1 *Character profiles* exercise.

Exercise 7.1a: Revolt

Scene 1

Think of someone who is really put upon by everyone else. If you have covered 8.1 *Character profiles*, it would be useful to think about your 'most repressed or enslaved' person.

- Describe that character in their normal routine. Tell us how they willingly put everyone else's needs ahead of theirs.
- During this time, something happens to make their situation much, much worse. Choose from Option A or Option B.

Option A: A new character arrives on the scene

- This new character might be their friend, a bully who makes even more demands upon your character.
- Or perhaps your character finally makes a new friend, who gives them the idea that it is about time that the bully got taught a lesson?

Option B: Some fact comes to light, that really upsets your character, and pushes them over the edge

- The bully might have started showing off about your character on a social networking site.
- Or your character might find out that the bully is going to get them thrown out of school.

Scene 2

- Your character tries to cope, but the new development makes it very difficult. Note that they really want to make life go on as before, but this desire is thwarted by the new circumstance.
- Finally, at the end of this scene, an event occurs which forces them to realize that they just cannot take it any more.

Scene 3

- Your character finally revolts.
- What happens?
- Is it successful or does the revolt fail?
- How does the revolt affect everybody?
- Are there any unexpected twists?

Note: this story is broken into two or more sections or scenes, and the total story may be several pages long, but remember – try to be as economical as possible.

Exercise 7.2b: Revenge

Scene 1

Introduce us to a person who is always the brunt of practical jokes (again, think about using your 'Most repressed or enslaved' person' if you have already done 8.1 *Character profiles*).

- Near the end of the scene, something happens that pushes him/her over the edge.
- At that moment, he/she decides to spring a practical joke of his/her own to get even.

Scene 2

The main character makes preparations for the joke:

- Does he/she need to find helpers, secure a location, and gather props?
- The scene ends when he/she is all set to spring the joke.

Scene 3

The main character springs the joke.

- What happens as a result?
- Can you come up with a twist, for example the joke has some unexpected or undesired effect?

Note: this story is broken into two or more sections or scenes, and the total story may be several pages long. But try to be as economical as possible.

Exercise 7.3c: Escape

Scene 1

Introduce us to a main character that, in the normal course of life, suddenly finds himself/herself in some sort of trap or prison.

This can be:

- A real, physical imprisonment (jail, a mine, a castle, a dungeon).
- A social situation (trapped at a very dull party, in a boring lesson, in a slow religious service).
- Possibly even some kind of mental prison, for example, someone with a phobia about spiders is stuck in a corner of their bedroom because there is a spider between them and the door.

Scene 2

The main character prepares an escape, plans it, and perhaps makes a preliminary attempt.

- They run into obstacles or setbacks, which make the situation worse.
- They must now adjust their plan accordingly.
- At the end of this part of the story, things have deteriorated and it seems they will never be able to escape. They decide to make one last try.

Scene 3

The main character makes their final, desperate attempt.

- What happens as a result? Did they escape? Was it a total success? A mixed success? A failure?
- Can you come up with a twist?

Note: this story is broken into two or more sections or scenes, and the total story may be several pages long. But try to be as economical as possible

Step 1: Classroom discussion – contexts

Take the time to lead a discussion about examples of stories and films that include one or more of the *Revolt, revenge, escape* scenarios. Your pupils can be encouraged to add to the following list.

Examples from fiction and film

- *Caspar* is an example of revolt: this little ghost refuses to be an evil ghost and goes against the rules of his ghostly colleagues by being friendly to a human.
- *Harry Potter* gets revenge, for his parents, and frequently upon Malfoy, and the Dursleys. Harry Potter often has to escape from physical traps, for example, being trapped with a giant snake, or inside a horrifying maze. The *Harry Potter* books also include examples of revolt, for example when the new headmistress who replaces Albus Dumbledore at Hogwarts introduces horrible new rules at the school.
- In *The Little Mermaid*, the heroine has the chance to escape and become a human, but only if she makes a man declare his love for her.
- In *Mrs Doubtfire*, the father, who is only allowed to see his children once a week, revolts against the court decision by dressing as a woman and becoming a nanny, thereby seeing his children every day.
- In *The Princess Bride*, at some stage all the characters have to escape from tough situations, revolt against the rules of the country, or get revenge upon an evil ruler.
- The first two *Home Alone* films feature many scenes of revenge and escape, from the thieves.
- In *101 Dalmatians*, the escape is from Cruella De Vil. In the film version, the dogs also get a wonderful revenge upon Cruella.
- *James and the Giant Peach*, *Oliver*, *Billy Elliot* and many other stories involve characters that must escape from awful situations, or revolt from them, or get their revenge upon tormentors.
- In *Pirates of the Caribbean*, Jack Sparrow must escape from jail.
- In the *Scooby Doo* stories, the cowardly dog and his friend, Shaggy, must always try to escape from a ghost or a pretend ghost.

Step 2: Pair work – character work

Children can break into pairs to come up with some ideas they have for the scenario of their choice, and the kind of character they are thinking of using. Get the children to talk about some of the following questions:

- How are you going to set up the main character's problems right at the start?
- You have only one scene to do this in. What props, actions or other clues can you come up with to show who this person is and how they get on with those around them, without relying totally on dialogue, or what the person says? (More detail about this was covered in Chapters 4 and 5.)
- Who is the most important person in the story at that moment?
- The person with the greatest desire will dominate a scene. Thus in *101 Dalmations*, when Cruella de Vil meets the Dalmation puppies, her desire for a spotted fur coat dominates the scene, rather than any joy that the dogs or owners feel about the arrival of the puppies. When the children, in *Hansel and Gretel*, pretend that they are very thin, when the witch checks up on whether or not they are ready to eat, it is the witch's desire to eat roasted fat children that dominates the story. (This again was covered in Chapters 4 and 5.)
- Can you reduce each line of conversation or dialogue to the one-word verb underlying it (for example, attack, deflect, persuade, seduce)?
- This may not happen when you first pour the story down on the page, but look at your first draft and see if you can do it. If there are no underlying verbs (other than explaining, which is too emotionally neutral), is there enough conflict in the scene? (The use of dialogue was covered in 5.2 *Persuasion: unexpected arrival.*)
- Since you're working with three (or more) scenes, are there any opportunities for planting or pay-off? For example, the repressed character could have a favourite teddy or toy that the bully destroys, and this is the final straw. The trapped person could have some little thing that makes them feel safe – and when this thing is taken away, the trapped person is forced to act. The bullied person could have one shred of dignity left, and when this is taken away, they are forced to get revenge.

Start writing!

Pupils should be given time to complete the exercise and then share their work and provide feedback.

You may find it helpful to post the following questions up on the IWB in case anyone gets stuck or needs some help.

Questions to help your writing

Remember the earlier exercises, for example:

1 Where are your characters? What is the atmosphere? Can we tell anything about them from what they own, wear, or are decorated with? You can use ideas that you developed in 4.1 *Building atmosphere*, 4.2 *Sharing a room*, 4.3 *Getting ready for a date* and 4.4 *The character in the environment.*

2 Are there any opportunities for planting any object, and having a pay-off?

3 Economy in dialogue: the way characters talk in stories and films is designed, mostly, to sound realistic, but it is not.

A 'real life' piece of dialogue might go like this:

> Julie said, 'What a lovely blue jumper.'
> Bob replied, 'Oh this old thing?'
> 'But it really suits you.'
> Bob answered, 'No, no, I just picked it up off the floor this morning.'
> 'Honestly it is great, where did you get it?'

And so on. In real life we can take our time in getting to the point and repeat ourselves a lot.

In a short story, this dialogue would be changed or cut to tell us what was really going on in a much more economical way.

> 'What a gorgeous jumper,' Julie lied. Uncle Bob puffed out his chest and checked his reflection in the hallway mirror. It was working.

Julie knew that Uncle Bob couldn't resist flattery and she wanted the keys to his sports car for the weekend.

Note also in the second version of the dialogue, a little conflict has been added. Julie has plans for Uncle Bob's car, goals that probably conflict with Uncle Bob's plans for the weekend. Conflict creates interest in a story.

Step 3: Giving feedback

Feedback should follow guidelines laid out in 4.5 *Giving feedback*. As pupils read each other's work they can be reminded to ask themselves the following questions.

Feedback reminder

You should understand, as you read the work of other pupils:

- Who is the main character?
- Why do they want to revolt, get revenge from, or escape from the situation/other character?
- What obstacles stand in their way?
- What happened in the end?

Summary

This exercise provides students with another classical story template and they should now be able to identify many favourite stories that are based upon this, and thus be better equipped to deconstruct complex plots, and to create their own multilayered plot lines.

Pupils can also use this exercise as a transformative tool with which to view their own personal life stories. They will now understand that the fabric of their own lives can be used as the foundation of a piece of fiction, but they have the ability to transform the endings of personal stories that did not end so very well. Pupils can likewise change the endings of horrible stories that they have come across in news media or on TV.

7.2 The world of the story

Introduction

The following questions are intended as a starting point for all the more advanced exercises, from this section onwards. While not designed to generate a story on their own, the questions in this exercise can be used to develop and enrich any ideas that pupils come up with for writing of their own, independent of the scenarios in this book.

These questions also help to prepare pupils writing earlier exercises and should be saved, as answering the questions during the drafting stage will help pupils in all future creative and non-fiction writing.

Step 1: Classroom discussion – background work

First explain the reasons why it is important to work on the background to a story.

Remember that stories, films and even games are selective: we get a glimpse into the lives of people, but we never see the whole of their lives. We see the tip of the iceberg, but the bulk remains unseen – though it is implied.

Your storytelling will be richer if you base it upon the sturdy foundation of a well-thought-out world – the back-story to your character's lives.

Pupils may be able to add to the following list of examples.

Examples from fiction and film

- The *Harry Potter* books begin with Harry living at the Dursleys – we do not hear all about every day of his life up to the time he gets into Hogwarts.
- We read about *Robin Hood* robbing the rich – we do not find out his whole life story.

- We read about *Nancy Drew* trying to solve mysteries – we do not have to read her whole life story up until she starts trying to be a detective.
- We meet *Shrek* living alone in his swamp – we never find out who his mother and father were or what his life was like up until then.

Step 2: Individual or pair work – characters

Although the writer usually includes only the information that we need to understand the story, they will usually have completed some background work to develop the characters, and would be able to answer all the questions listed below about their characters.

Think of a character that you have already written about, or one that you might want to write about in your next story. (See 8.1 *Character profiles* for more examples.) You could also get your pupils to answer these questions with reference to a well-known character from a book studied or read in class.

Children can try to answer the questions below in pairs or as a whole class, with a teacher noting answers on a board.

Step 3: Pair work – choose your story

Pupils now need to select a story idea that they have worked upon in class already, one that they feel has the potential to be crafted into a successful, longer piece.

This could be one of the templates from Chapter 6, for example, 6.1 *The love story* or 6.3 *The caper*. It could be the outline just covered in 7.1 *Revolt, revenge, escape* or be based upon one of the earlier exercises, such as 4.2 *Sharing a room* or 5.2 *Persuasion: unexpected arrival*.

Pupils can discuss ways to answer the list of questions above, using the characters from their selected story idea.

Start writing!

You may find it helpful to post the following questions up on the IWB in case anyone gets stuck or needs some help.

Questions to help your writing

1   What is your character's routine? What time do they typically get up? Go to sleep? Who do they share their home with, if at all?

2   Who do they meet on a regular basis? Is there anyone that they try to avoid on a regular basis?

3   Where do they work, play, or go for most of the day? What is their school, home or working routine like? How often do they see the head teacher or boss – and how do they get on with this person? What about co-workers or classmates? Younger pupils or staff they have to manage?

4   If your character is a student or pupil, what classes do they take? Which class or activity do they dread? Which one do they look forward to? Do they have any interests or outside activities?

5   What hobbies are part of their daily life? Playing computer games, football, swimming, dancing, hunting, fishing, playing cards, knitting?

6   Who are the most powerful people in your character's life? Who is in charge? Are there any characters in their life that are bossed around by them? Do religious beliefs or social customs affect your character? Is there any kind of political situation in their life, or do local or national politics affect your character?

7   How about the place where your character lives? Is it a little village, a town, a big city? Is it one of those towns where everyone works on a farm, or for the local theme park? How does the way the area makes its money affect the local population? Are they all old miners who have lost their jobs, or young people who work in shops?

8   What kind of neighbours does your character have? Are they rich, middling or poor? Do they have twenty tattoos or teeth missing? Are they all really fat, or really religious, or nosy?

9   What about the weather? Cloudy? Stormy? Always sunny?

Step 4: Giving feedback

Feedback should follow guidelines laid out in 4.5 *Giving feedback*. As pupils read each other's work they can be reminded to ask themselves the following questions.

> **Feedback reminder**
>
> You should understand, as you read the work of other pupils:
>
> - Who is this character?
> - What kind of problems do they have in life?
> - What kind of person are they?
> - Do you like this person?
> - Why does the author want to write about this character?
> - Can you describe what they look like, just from what you have read?

Summary

Beginning writers, in their eagerness to tell what they believe is an exciting, adventure-filled plot, can easily forget to do adequate preparatory work, particularly into their characters. The result can be a disappointing story filled with action, but based upon characters that no one cares about. Most children (and adults) may have seen this type of story or film.

Children can also tend to base their stories upon characters pretty much like themselves or even think that providing such detail is not needed. On the contrary, such detail is what a story depends upon. First, young writers must learn to complete enough preparatory work so that they have a strong sense of exactly who their characters are. Second, they must learn to drip-feed some of this background detail into their stories to enrich the text.

Examples of these techniques are routinely found in the work of their favourite authors, for example:

- What would Harry Potter be without the room under the stairs, and his awful relatives, the Dursleys?

- Can you imagine Ron Weasley without his redheaded family, or Hermione Granger without her dentist parents?
- How could we enjoy a film about an ugly ogre who wants to be alone, without the opening scenes of *Shrek*, where we see him take a shower, eat dinner alone, and go about his daily business?

All of these pieces of extra information about our favourite characters have been included in the story for a particular reason: to help us engage, empathize and to let us know how unique the characters are. This background information helps us to develop affection and understanding for the characters, to enjoy following their adventures, and to make us keep reading or watching.

This exercise puts the onus firmly upon pupils to get the groundwork done before launching into a longer piece of work. Pupils begin to understand that a story does not form, fully created, in a writer's pen as they sit at their desk. A story can now be understood as beginning with the creation of multilayered characters, and being dependent upon a structure that must rest upon very solid foundations.

7.3 Story questions

Introduction

This section provides a list of core story questions that can be used in many ways as the basis for developing stories:

- It can be used at the planning stage of multiple writing formats – a writing assignment, an essay, a story, a poem or a play. In this case, the handout can be projected on the IWB, and the teacher can ask pupils to generate ideas as to how each question could be answered.
- It can be used to help pupils understand any text. For example, if pupils are trying to work out how Roald Dahl's story, *The Twits*, works, the teacher can stimulate discussion and gauge pupils' comprehension by asking pupils to apply these questions to the text. This exercise can help pupils develop a better understanding of

how their favourite stories work, and of the structure that is built into them.

- More confident writers can be given this list of questions in paper form, to use for their own reference, either in the planning of a story, or during the writing of a story, to provide assistance any time they get stuck.
- Once the explanations behind the questions have been discussed, pupils will be able to use the shorter version (below) to help with a range of writing assignments.

Pupils need to work through the list of questions, together or in small groups, writing down their answers as they go. If they can answer the questions below, before they begin writing, or even if they get stuck later on, they will find they have a very strong foundation upon which to base their stories.

Question 1: Whose story is it?

A great story is never about a wishy-washy, average, too familiar person, who kind of wants something but does not really care that much, who never gets around to getting it, and who we do not really even like very much. If you can work out the answers to this list of questions, you will be on your way to creating a really excellent piece of writing.

Who is your main character (or protagonist)? If you ask your pupils what their favourite stories are, they will almost always tell you about the main character – this is where the story begins for most of us. A good story is about a clearly defined character, who we care about.

The protagonist is the character whose needs and desires shape the action of the story and everything that happens in it. You need to know who this is before you start.

You should be able to get pupils to add to the following list.

Examples from fiction and film

- The grumpy old man in the film *Up* wants to float his house down to South America on a journey that he had wanted to take with his wife, who has recently died.

> - Brer Rabbit always wants to outwit Brer Bear, Fox and so on.
> - Cinderella wants to go to the ball.
> - Prince Caspian wants to save Narnia.
> - Luke Skywalker wants to outwit the Empire.

Sometimes it might seem that a story has several main characters. But if you look closely, you will find that the focus is nearly always on one character. For example, even though Hermione and Ron support Harry, the *Harry Potter* books are about him, and if someone asked you what the books were about, you might begin by answering that they are about a boy, called Harry, who finds out that he is a wizard.

Often the story is named after the main character; this can be seen with *Jack and the Beanstalk*, *Little Red Riding Hood* and *Charlie and the Chocolate Factory*.

In other stories you might have a group of characters chasing the same goal – for example, in *The Spiderwick Chronicles* or *Narnia*. In these cases, the main character will be the one who is changed the most by the experiences they have gone through during the course of the story.

There are exceptions to the importance of a main character. There are some stories where the author has chosen to have a group of characters – the *Famous Five*, *Secret Seven* and *Swallows and Amazons* are examples of this kind of story. However, these kinds of stories are in the minority. Writing for a group is more complicated, and as beginning writers it will be simpler for pupils to start by creating stories where they can easily say who their main character is. Even if you now know who your main character is, you must also be able to explain what is special about your character.

Question 2: Why are you interested in this character?

- What is the special problem that this character has that you would like to explore through writing this story?
- Be sure to think not only about this character, but also about their world – what is their daily routine?
- Who are their friends?
- Work colleagues?
- Fellow pupils or students?

You need to have enough interest in this character, and care enough about their particular problems and flaws, to be able to generate the same level of interest in us, your readers.

For example, if your story is about a boy who has to kill lots of monsters, then you already have a plot with some action in it, and the monsters should make it exciting. But readers will not care about the boy or the monsters unless some time has been spent working out exactly who the boy is, and what kind of problems he faces in defeating the monsters. If the boy lives with his awful Aunty Margaret, on a sheep farm, because his mother has run away to be on *The X Factor*, and his aunt has no idea that the boy has to leave the farm every night to kill the monsters who are out to eat all her sheep, then perhaps we have the beginnings of a more interesting story.

Our characters are defined by the relationships we have with those closest to us.

- Who does your character love or like the most?
- Who do they hate?
- Are they subservient, or bossed about?
- Or are they usually the one in control, the leader in any social situation?
- Is your character trusting of others? Or cynical?

Question 3: What does your main character want?

What is your character's goal in life? The main character's desire for something or some objective is the engine that drives the main tension of the story and keeps your readers wanting to find out what happens.

Your main character's need to achieve their objective creates the main tension and shape of the story. The stronger the desire, the more intense and gripping your story will be.

Examples from fiction and film

- A good example of this is found across the whole of the *Harry Potter* series where Harry's desire to defeat Voldemort shapes the action of seven books.

- In the *Dr Who* series and the *Sarah Jane Adventures*, the main characters must defeat a succession of aliens who threaten life on earth, but they are often hampered by the fact that they have to follow certain universal laws about time, and must not let 'normal' humans in their lives, like teachers and parents, know about the aliens.

Question 4: What is at stake?

- If your main character does not get what they want, what will happen?
- What price will be paid?

If nothing much will happen either way, and the result will have no effect on the character's feelings or upon the success of their lives, in terms of money or love, or any other goals, then it will be difficult to create any tension in the story, or to get your readers involved in it.

Question 5: What is the main tension?

- What is the main tension that you want your readers to feel as they turn the pages?
- The main tension, or problem, can be called the 'central dramatic question'. Can you write out the central dramatic question of your story?

Examples from fiction and film

- Will Harry Potter defeat Voldemort?
- Will Little Red Riding Hood outwit the wolf?
- Will the Big Bad Wolf eat the Three Little Pigs?
- Will Shrek succeed in getting back to his swamp to live all alone?

Question 6: Where is 'hope versus fear'

- As we read your story, we should be hoping that your character will succeed and be very afraid what might happen if they don't succeed.
- Have you considered any wrong turns the story could possibly take? Both results – the ending we are hoping for as we read, and the one we fear as we read – must be possible to create a good, strong, tension that will keep us turning the pages.
- If life is just too easy for your main character, and you fail to keep us fearful and hopeful, then you are also failing to keep us interested.
- Try to write down what you want your readers to hope, and also to fear, as they read your story.

Examples from fiction and film

- If we know all along that Harry will defeat Voldemort and it never looks as if he will fail, then why read any more?
- If we know all along that the Big Bad Wolf will end up cooked in a pot, why bother reading any further?

Question 7: What is the life dream of your character?

- If your main character could change the world, what would be their ideal world?
- What do they think life would be like for them if they achieved this world?
- What would they dream a perfect life to be like for themselves?

This life dream may be beyond the scope of the story.

Examples from fiction and film

- The Big Bad Wolf just wants to eat dinner; he may dream of an endless supply of juicy young pigs, but that never happens.
- Harry Potter, in each book, has one separate goal – while he might dream of defeating Voldemort, in the mean time he just wants to get to Hogwarts, or stay out of trouble.

A character's life dream might be to:

- play football like a Premier League star
- travel to Mars
- be a great journalist
- defeat all evil in the world
- rid the world of wolves
- make everyone a vegetarian
- convert everyone to their religious beliefs.

But what they want in the story could just to be to:

- play football on the local team without falling in the mud
- visit an observatory
- write a story for the school newspaper
- catch a neighbourhood thief
- visit the wolf sanctuary in the local zoo
- cook one vegetarian meal for their dad
- sit through one sermon in the church.

Try to write down what you think the life dream of your character could be.

Question 8: How does your character change during the story?

If your story is about a comic character, see the important note below.

In many of the best stories, the main character will end up, emotionally, in the opposite place to where they started.

Examples from fiction and film

- Thus Cinderella starts out as a scullery maid and ends up as a princess.
- The cowboy in *Toy Story* starts out in a box of unwanted toys.
- Shrek starts out as a grumpy ugly ogre who wants to be left alone.
- The teenage girl in *The Princess Diaries* just wants to be a normal girl.

The difference between how a character starts out and where they end up at the end of a story is also called the character arc, or character polarity, by professional writers. This describes how your main character can virtually move, emotionally, from the North Pole to the South Pole during a story, in the opposite place to where they started.

Examples from fiction and film

- Shrek starts out wanting to be alone in his swamp and ends up in the polar opposite position – in love with, and happily married to, Princess Fiona.
- In *The Spiderwick Chronicles*, the children are upset that their parents are getting a divorce and the first goal of one of the boys is not to defeat the magical creatures that surround their new home, but simply to get his dad back with his mum.
- Harry Potter's first goal is to get away from his awful relatives and succeed in getting into Hogwarts School, and he ends up a lot further along from this simple goal by the end of the series.
- In *How to Lose a Guy in 10 Days*, the heroine's goal is to get the hero to break up with her – and she ends up in the polar opposite position, very much in love with the man.

Can you describe how your character is changed, psychologically or emotionally, by the story? Have they been transformed in any really profound or meaningful way?

If you are planning to write about a character that will not change much, how can the circumstances of the story be changed to better explore the weaknesses or problems that your character might have when the story begins? Good stories are very hard to create if they are based upon almost perfect characters, leading perfect lives, easily achieving their dreams.

Is there a need that the character could be totally unaware of at the start, while they are busy trying to achieve something else? For example, a little girl whose goal in life is to win a beauty competition might realize that what she really needs is some friends; a boy whose goal is to avoid being bullied might realize that what he really needs to do is find his father. A child who wants to win the Nobel Prize for Peace might realize that he/she just wants to make their family get on better.

Does the story help the character to finally discover what it is that they really need the most? If the character does not undergo any sort of change or transformation the story is probably too easy on the character. Can you find ways to make it any harder?

Note about comic characters

A comic character (not a character caught up in a comic situation, but rather a character that is intrinsically comical, such as Donald Duck, Tom in *Tom and Jerry*, Mr Bean, Wile E. Coyote, Dennis the Menace, Basil Fawlty) and a comic-book character will never undergo the kind of transformation described above, in a story – because that is the key to their comic effect. No matter what happens, they will never learn, and never stop making the mistakes that make us laugh at them.

Question 9: What is your theme?

It should be possible to express a theme in a few words. Try to work out how to say in the simplest, and shortest way, what is your story about? This can be Trust – Greed – Responsibility – Self-acceptance – Generosity – Love, and so on.

Pupils can have a go at working out the themes of some of their favourite stories.

Examples from fiction and film

- *Harry Potter* – unconditional love defeats evil
- *Star Wars* – a son's fight with his dad
- *High School Musical* – creating something great through working together
- *The Lord of the Rings* – the price of defeating evil
- *Penelope* – self-acceptance
- *A Christmas Carol* – generosity
- *Shrek* – love conquers all.

Pupils can be challenged to come up with stories that they believe have no theme. You could also ask pupils to come up with the themes for some of these well-known stories:

- *Robin Hood*
- *The Three Little Pigs*
- *Hansel and Gretel*
- *Jack and the Beanstalk*
- *The Elves and the Shoemaker*

Often the theme is carried by the main character or protagonist – they are unaware of some truth at the outset of the story, but the rigours of the adventure that they set out upon force them into a new awareness, often at the moment of greatest stress. Once you have the answers to these questions, you will have an extremely solid foundation upon which to build a story.

If you have answered these questions about a favourite text, you will also have a very clear idea of how it was planned and the kinds of preparation that the author did before they wrote the story.

Sometimes it is very difficult to work out the exact theme of your story before you write it. In cases like this it is better to have a rough form of 'working theme' or an idea of what the theme may be, and to revise it as you go along.

Review of the task before pupils start writing

Having done the preliminary work, children can be reminded of the exercise. Take time to go over the following guidance with them.

Guidance

Your pupils will be ready to either

- Apply the list of questions to their own favourite texts
- Apply the list of questions to one of their own story ideas.

Start writing!

You may find it helpful to post the following questions up on the IWB in case anyone gets stuck or needs some help.

Questions to help your writing

Story questions – short version

1   Whose story is it?
2   Why are you interested in this character?
3   What does your main character want?
4   What is at stake?
5   What is the main tension?
6   Where is 'hope versus fear'?
7   What is the life dream of your character?
8   How does your character change during the story?
9   What is your theme?

Giving feedback

Feedback should follow guidelines laid out in 4.5 *Giving feedback*. As pupils read each other's work they can be reminded to ask themselves the following questions.

Feedback reminder

You should understand, as you read the work of other pupils:

- Who is the character?
- What do they want in life?
- What parts of their personality might make life difficult for them?
- What is their main influence in life?
- Why are you interested in this character?
- How are they going to be changed by what has happened during the story?

Summary

This exercise is best illustrated with examples generated by the pupils themselves, drawn from their own experience of written or filmed texts. Questions in the template are open-ended in structure, allowing you to provide further examples generated from your own recent reading and viewing.

Pupils might be resistant to the concept that all great stories have been built upon the kind of foundation generated by these questions, and their resistance should be acknowledged. Clearly, not all stories are based upon such templates but certainly many do follow such structures. During classroom discussion it will, however, become apparent that pupils already have strong ideas as to what their favourite stories are, and from this, they will be able to work out those elements that should be present in the best stories, and in their own.

Creating a story is similar to setting out on a very long journey. As beginning writers, the long journey will be made much easier if pupils have made good preparations and some solid plans about how they are going to get where they want to go. Some writers do just sit down and write, and work out what is going to happen as they go along. For example, Chilean novelist Isabel Allende starts a book by pouring the writing down onto the page and a first draft of a novel could be over 900 pages. She would then cut these pages down to 200 and start again, rewriting and letting her characters emerge as she writes. The final version of a novel, which might be 300 pages long, and over ten drafts later, could have been cut from many thousands of pages of original writing.

Pupils should be made aware that they are being offered a toolkit of writing techniques. They can adapt these templates for their own use; they will find some exercises really excite them and some, they will find dull. Children can learn to concentrate upon the ideas that work best for them. If, as a child's writing becomes more sophisticated, they choose to disregard the techniques described here and substitute them with their own creative style, then this is a perfectly natural and acceptable development.

Some writers begin with a very clear idea of who their central character is, and then spend a long time developing a complicated plot, before starting to write. Other writers struggle to get a first line down. Virginia Woolf famously worked very hard to create the first line of her novel, *Mrs Dalloway*. In Dodie Smith's novel, *I Capture the Castle*, a writer is locked in a tower and writes one line over and over again in an attempt to get started on a story.

This book is designed to provide support, guidance and encouragement to young, beginning writers as they set out upon their work. The exercises are designed to remove the fear of a blank page for writers, and to encourage them to commence the work of writing a story with sufficient preparatory and background work that the story can flow directly from the preparatory work. The theory that underpins the exercises in this book is built upon a firm belief that it is possible to teach pupils a range of techniques that are transferable to multiple writing formats. The templates within this book have been used at major film schools and in university creative writing degree programmes to successfully help generations of writers achieve their dreams, and to create compelling stories.

Resources for following many more alternative paths to creativity, and expanding upon the exercises in this book, are to be found in every good bookstore. However two of the best of these books are listed below:

- *The Artist's Way* by Julia Cameron (1997, Pan).
- *Writing Down the Bones* by Natalie Goldberg (2005, Shambala).

7.4   Freytag's Triangle

Introduction

This section provides questions that will help your pupils to develop an understanding of story structure. This structure can be used in many ways, as described in 7.3 *Story question:* Introduction.

Step 1: Classroom discussion – the game of the story

Story structure is best explained when illustrated by examples derived from an existing, well-known story, so that your pupils have a practical demonstration of how this structure actually works.

For the sake of illustration we have chosen to discuss the story structure of the first Harry Potter book, *Harry Potter and the Philosopher's Stone*, as we have found a universal awareness of the plot of this book among primary school pupils. Another text can be substituted, at the teacher's discretion.

The goal of the first moments of your story is to hook into your readers' emotions. You need to create tension by playing with your readers' very best hopes for your character and their very worst fears for your character. To make this work well, you will need a main character with whom your readers can empathize, sympathize and understand, to some degree.

Example
When we first meet Harry Potter:
• We find out about his life with the dreadful Dursleys.

> • Harry has to sleep in the cupboard under the stairs because his awful cousin Dudley needs a second bedroom for the incredible number of toys and gifts that he has been spoiled with.
> • We find out that Harry never gets any presents from this family.

This information helps readers to understand Harry's character and to empathize with him in his struggles with the Dursleys, to the extent that during a visit to the zoo, when a snake seems to chase Dudley out of the reptile house, we are very much on Harry's side.

Once there is an emotional bond between your readers and your main character, the stresses, strains, tests, obstacles and adventures of your main character will now have an emotional effect upon your readers. Ready, set, *go*!

Step 2: Classroom discussion – trials and tribulations

Freytag's Triangle was defined by Gustav Freytag (1816–1895), a German novelist and dramatist. It is a practical way of arranging your main character's adventures so that they will have the greatest effect on your readers (see diagram).

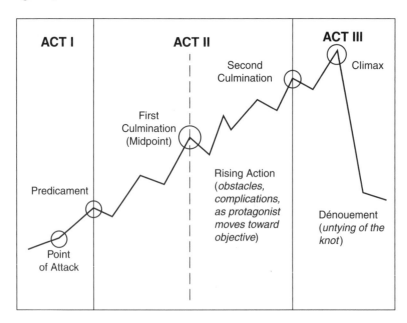

The jagged, rising line is a measure of the amount of tension generated in your readers, derived from their hopes and fears about the results of the main character's adventures. You can use this diagram to try to arrange the events in your story. The major elements of the Triangle are described below with illustrations that your pupils can easily add to.

The character has been described going about their daily routine or life so that we are engaged with them. Now a problem comes about that demands your main character's attention. The problem should also threaten to disturb their daily life and habits.

This is known as the *point of attack* or inciting incident by writers. It describes an event or a moment that happens which changes the direction of your main character's life. Before this moment, the main character's life would have continued as before. After this event, the course of their life is changed forever.

This event alone does not tell us what the story will be about, but it does give us a very clear hint at the direction that the story will take from now on.

Example

Harry Potter is living under the staircase at the Dursleys' house, just trying to survive his childhood, when he tags along on Dudley's birthday outing to the zoo, only because his uncle and aunt cannot leave him behind. While at the zoo, Harry manages to talk to a snake and release it. After this moment, nothing will ever be the same. The incident at the zoo does not tell us about the central theme of the book, the fight to defeat Voldemort, but it does give us a good idea about the direction that the story will now take.

Step 3: Classroom discussion – the big dilemma

The big dilemma is also called the *predicament*, or the end of Act I. Whatever happened at the point of attack had led to a situation that the main character must confront and solve. Normally it is a situation that contains a dilemma, or a 'damned if you do, damned if you don't' moment.

A dilemma is perfectly demonstrated in a 1950s movie *Return to the Forbidden Planet*. Robbie the robot is ordered by his master and creator to fire his weapon upon some humans who have visited the planet. However Robbie has been programmed to:

- always obey his master and
- never fire upon a human

After getting his master's orders, Robbie lifts his weapon, points it at the humans, then rocks to and fro, all his circuits catch fire, and he malfunctions. The dilemma has destroyed his circuits.

When we ask each other, 'What is your story about?' or 'What is that book or film about?' the answer is usually based upon the predicament.

Example

Harry Potter is determined to read the letter that has come through the post, inviting him to take up a place at Hogwarts School. His step-parents take fairly extreme steps to stop Harry getting this letter, as they do not want to have anything to do with the magical world. Imprisoned in a remote lighthouse, Harry finally gets to read the letter offering him a place at Hogwarts, when it is delivered in person by a giant, called Hagrid. Harry must choose either to escape with the quite frightening giant, Hagrid, who has arrived to take him to Hogwarts, or stay with his awful relatives.

Step 4: Classroom discussion – the midpoint

The *midpoint* is also called *first culmination*, and is in the middle of Act II. In feature film construction, there is often a midpoint culmination that profoundly affects the direction of the story in some way. This may be a revelation or some reversal of fortune that makes the protagonist's task more difficult. Sometimes this is a mirror image of the culmination, a moment of apparent triumph before disaster occurs.

Example

During a Quidditch match, Harry Potter's broomstick goes out of control and he nearly dies. Harry's friends, believing that Professor Snape is trying to kill Harry, attack Snape to stop him muttering a spell, setting his cloak on fire. Harry and his two friends then overhear further conversations between Snape and Professor Quirrel that convince them that Snape is trying to get hold of the philosopher's stone.

Sometimes this moment resolves the tension begun at the predicament, but the solution leads to a new and even more desperate complication that must now be solved. Another example is that, when trying to rescue a unicorn in the forbidden forest, the three friends find out that the philosopher's stone could help Lord Voldemort to make the elixir of life and so regain his full powers.

Step 5: Classroom discussion – rising action

This is what happens throughout the whole story – tension builds, layer is added to layer, the drama escalates and we keep turning the pages. When the Harry Potter books were first published, some children would queue up all day to get a copy and then stay up all night, for perhaps many nights, until they had finished reading it.

Sometimes when you are at the cinema, or watching a movie at home, you might need to run to the loo – but you cannot leave your seat. And some pupils will have had stories read to them, in class or at home, and begged for the person reading to keep going: 'Just one more page – please?'

If this has happened to you, you know that 'rising action' has had you trapped in the story, wanting to know what happens next. If the story has a good structure, you will never have to worry about 'rising action' because it will be built in. The only time you will notice this element is if it is missing – if you are writing about a happy person with no problems and a wonderful life, for example. But after using the exercises in this book there is no chance that would ever, ever, happen. Right?

Step 6: Classroom discussion – end of Act II

The *second culmination* is sometimes known as the *low point*: it is the lowest point in the whole story, except in a tragedy, in which case it is a *high point*. As the protagonist strives towards their objective, this is often the moment at which it appears all is lost. It gives us a glimpse as to how the story might have gone. This is often the point in the story in which the main tension is resolved, but, like the first culmination, it leads to an even more desperate situation, which initiates a whole new tension for Act III.

Example

At this point in the story Harry realizes that the Chamber of Secrets, where the philosopher's stone is hidden, is no longer secure because Hagrid has told a stranger in a pub the secret of making the three-headed dog that guards the stone go to sleep. Dumbledore is away and Harry and his friends must enter the Chamber of Secrets.

Step 7: Classroom discussion – the climax

In the *climax*, the main character's final desperate attempt to achieve their objective or goal leads to a moment of truth, which then leads to the ending. The problem that began with the predicament/dilemma at the end of Act I has now been solved, for good or for bad. Often, in a really good story, the ending has some kind of twist.

Example

In the Chamber of Secrets, Harry confronts Professor Quirrel, who demands the philosopher's stone, and admits that he has been taken over by Lord Voldemort. The stone falls into Harry's pocket but when Quirrel/Voldemort tries to grab it, he is burned.

Step 8: Classroom discussion – the ending

The ending is also sometimes called the *dénouement*.

After all the tension of the story, this is a moment when you can let your readers revisit characters, tie up loose ends, and in general let us down from the high of finding out what happened before we close the book, leave the characters and your story behind, and get back to the real world.

> **Example**
>
> Harry awakes in the school hospital, where Dumbledore tells him that he survived because his mother sacrificed her life to protect him, and Voldemort could not understand the power of such love. Voldemort left Quirrell to die, and is likely to return by some other means. The philosopher's stone has now been destroyed. Harry returns to the Dursleys for the summer holiday, but does not tell them that under-age wizards are forbidden to use magic outside Hogwarts.

CHAPTER 8

The satisfying ending

Introduction

Chapters 6, 7 and 8 enable children to build upon fundamental skills developed through the earlier chapters. It is possible to use the templates within these chapters as stand-alone writing exercises, but it is assumed that children at this stage will have fairly well-developed writing skills, including the ability to create strong characters and obstacles and the ability to employ atmosphere and environment effectively. Reference to earlier exercises that can enrich work for the later chapters is cited where relevant. The layout of Chapters 6, 7 and 8 is simpler, because it is assumed that pupils will not need to be helped to develop fundamental story components before moving on to develop the entire narrative.

In this chapter we open with Exercise 8.1, which is used to generate *Character profiles*: this will help pupils create a list of archetypal characters that can be used throughout their writing.

This is followed by three story templates to complete the series begun in earlier chapters:

- 8.2 *The supernatural*
- 8.3 *The threat to world views*
- 8.4 *Journey with destination*

Finally, 8.5 *The escape* will enable pupils to transfer abilities developed through completing the templates in this book into multiple writing formats.

The templates are designed to generate outlines that can be used to create sustained, longer fiction. Creating an outline provides pupils with a solid understanding of the way such templates work. Children will be able to bring their understanding of the way these fundamental templates work to help with the development of their own fiction.

In this chapter, outlines are being used because the plots generated will be sufficient to support a complete story or even a novel or a film. Pupils can be asked to complete the stories based upon these templates in their own time, or class time can be set aside to enable pupils to write out the whole text.

8.1 Character profiles

Introduction

The character profiles worked on in this exercise will enable pupils to create strong, compelling characters that will be useful in all the exercises in this book and in any other writing that they do. The characters generated by this exercise are extremes, and it is their very strong characteristics that make them useful in fiction. However, pupils may also identify qualities in people close to themselves, or even within their own personalities.

This chapter emphasizes that character is story, and these exercises provide a springboard to more engaging storytelling.

Exercise 8.1: Character profiles

Most ambitious person

Write a half to one page description of the most ambitious person you know – make sure it is someone you know personally. What is this person prepared to do, to give up, to overcome, to achieve their ambitions? Provide at least one specific example (preferably more) of a behaviour or situation you witnessed or heard about which expresses the character's ambition – examples that might help someone who doesn't know him/her to get sense of the person. Do you have any ideas about why this person is this way – what might have shaped him/her?

Character least capable of love

Write a half to one page profile on a person you know whom you consider to be the least capable of love – this can be romantic love, love for a family member, friend or their pet. This is the kind of person, who, if an aunt came to visit and ran towards them for a big soppy kiss, would run a mile. Even if you snuggled up to them when you were watching a scary film at this person's house, they would probably squirm away from you. Can you think of any specific examples of this person's behaviour that expresses this quality? Any ideas about why this person is the way he/she is – what might have made him/her behave this way?

Most repressed or enslaved person

Write a half to one page profile of the most repressed or enslaved person you know. This might be the child who always runs errands for the others, or gives them his/her pocket money, or gets made to do things they don't want to do, by other kids. It may be someone who is a 'doormat', allowing themselves to be run over by others; someone who quietly puts up with being a victim. Perhaps it is someone you know who has been bullied? Write down any specific examples of his or her behaviour that expresses this quality, so that a stranger would be able to get a sense of the person. Any ideas about why this person is the way he/she is – what might have made them this way? What makes a person into a victim?

Most set in their ways

Write a half to one page profile of the person you know who is the most set in his/her ways – someone who would be the most threatened by any change in their life. This person would be upset if dinner was not at six o'clock precisely, or if their pencils were not in the right order on their desks. They might have to go on holiday to the same place every year, or always eat the same food each day, or keep all their toys in a set place. Write down any specific examples of his or her behaviour that expresses this quality, so that a stranger would be able to get sense of the person. Any ideas about why this person is the way they are? What makes a person feel safe if their routine is the same every day?

The biggest liar

Write a half to one page profile on the biggest liar you know or have known. This person will tell the most ridiculous lies – that their father is an undercover spy, that they came to school in a spaceship, that their uncle is a famous footballer, that they are getting a toy shop for Christmas. The lies are always really ridiculous but for some reason, they just keep on making them up. Can you think of any specific examples of the liar's behaviour that expresses this quality? Any ideas about why this person is the way he/she is – what might have shaped him/her?

The most spiritual or religious person

Write a half to one page profile on a person you know whom you consider to be the most spiritual or religious. This trait can be inspirational or it could be a bit silly. Do you have an aunt who sings along with her tambourine in the High Street to help bring her message to the shoppers? Or perhaps you have an uncle who prays almost all day, who you go and visit when you have a problem, because he always has the best advice? Do you have a cousin who has converted to a religion unfamiliar to your family? Do you come home from school to find your father cross-legged and meditating? An uncle who believes he has been kidnapped by aliens? Describe the person; give specific examples of how this person behaves, clues which lead you to your conclusion about their character. Any idea what makes them tick?

Tip

- The list of character types can be provided as a handout or given out to small groups within the class. The profiles would ideally be assigned at the rate of one per week, per pupil, during the early part of the course. However, there may not be enough weeks, or time, to assign all of the profiles. In this case, give pupils a choice.
- With a large class, short on time, a better option might be to allocate the character profiles evenly across the group so that every character

type can be presented or shared within groups once the exercise is completed.

- Students could complete the character profiles before doing 5.4 *Making a bad situation worse* or 7.1 *Revolt, revenge, escape*, when they will start using them in stories.

Step 1: Classroom discussion – examples

The following examples can be used if you feel pupils would benefit from finding out about how the archetypal characters generated through this exercise are employed by some of their favourite authors.

Examples from fiction and film

- J.K. Rowling's Voldemort is the epitome of evil – yet we learn to have some compassion for him. Harry Potter, his opponent, is not a perfect, fully developed wizard.
- J.R.R. Tolkein's Gollum is evil – yet it is only through developing some compassion for him, that Frodo ultimately defeats him and destroys the ring. Gollum's opponent, Frodo, is also flawed.
- In *Star Wars*, Luke Skywalker is ultimately a good character, and Darth Veda represents evil, yet their relationship is complex and spans six feature films. Neither character is perfect.
- The original fairytales of early childhood involve simple characters that are easy for infants to identify as representing forces of good or evil. These include *Cinderella*, the *Billy Goats Gruff*, *The Three Little Pigs*, *Little Red Riding Hood*, and so on.

As children get older and become more sophisticated, the stories created for them can involve more complex characters.

Contemporary authors are rewriting many classic stories for older audiences and in doing so they develop more nuanced, multilayered characters. Examples include:

- *Hoodwinked* is a feature film retelling the traditional story of *Little Red Riding Hood*, in which the wolf is innocent.

- *Ever After* is a feature film retelling of *Cinderella*, in which Cinderella, played by actress Drew Barrymore, is a tomboy.
- *Shrek* is a retelling of multiple children's fairy stories that allows for complex character development, in which the hero is an ugly ogre and the enemy is a charming prince.
- The *Mr Wolf* series retells many stories from the wolf's point of view.
- *The Gruffalo* is a story in which the standard confrontation with a monster is retold.

Encourage pupils to add to this list.

Step 2: Pair work – have you met these kinds of people?

- Ask children to read through the list of character profiles, and share stories about people they know, or characters from books and other media, who fit these profiles.
- Some of the stories could be useful in later classes; pupils can be encouraged to jot down notes about any stories they hear, or remember, that they like.
- Perhaps some pupils might realize that they share a few characteristics with some of these archetypes?

Step 3: Review of the task before pupils start writing

Having done the preliminary work, children can be reminded of the exercise. Take time to go over the following guidance with them.

Guidance

- Have someone in mind as you write each of the profiles.
- Keep it simple: you do not need to give a hundred examples of how your uncle is the biggest liar ever – just give us one occasion when it really got him into trouble.

> • Describe only what your readers could see and hear if they were there. If you write out the thoughts of your character, you are explaining the story to us rather than telling us the story. This gets boring. Your readers want to work it out for themselves.

Start writing!

You may find it helpful to post the character profiles up on the IWB in case anyone gets stuck or needs some help.

Step 4: Giving feedback

Feedback should follow guidelines laid out in Chapter 4.5. As pupils read each other's work they can be asked to consider whether or not they need more information, or if they know and understand these people from the descriptions given.

Summary

At this stage pupils are learning to acquire a 'magpie mind' – that is, to realize that almost everything is of use to them as young writers. They might hear a story about someone's eccentric uncle who is so very set in his ways that he had to have oxygen when his boiled egg was cooked the wrong way, or about someone who is so ambitious to become the next great sporting hero that they will never go to the beach, because it is a waste of valuable practice time. These stories can be added to by fellow pupils in the class or group and used to make their own stories stronger.

Your pupils may, at the start, be overly precious about their work and this exercise should help them to learn that in creative writing, other class members are there to help make their stories work. If a character based upon one pupil's ideas shows up in another pupil's story, however transformed, it should be taken as the highest form of flattery.

It is important to bear this in mind, particularly when pupils discuss the 'Most repressed or enslaved person'. There will be a chance, later on, for pupils to change the life of their characters around, to give them a very satisfying act of revolt or revenge against their oppressors.

At the end of this exercise, pupils will have a list of archetypal characters that can be used throughout their writing, though by the time the character has been written into a story by your classmate, he or she may not be recognizable.

For a writer, a certain satisfaction and even on occasions, revenge, can be derived from the knowledge that the most awkward situations and even painful experiences can be used at a later date, to make a story more satisfying. The annoying passenger on the train, who is giving away his life story by yelling into a mobile phone, can feature as a figure of fun in your next piece of work. The hypocritical, overweight older sister who employs a dog walker to take her fat, sad dog out, while she works out with a personal trainer, can help make your story really funny. The bossy man who shoved you out of the way to get on the rollercoaster ride can become stuck at the top of the biggest loop – for the night – in your very own horror story, later on.

Through this exercise pupils are being asked to use the stuff of their own lives as foundation stones for the creation of fiction. They can also begin to learn to become better observers of life, and collectors of the kinds of information that can greatly enrich their own work, and the work of others.

Pupils can also begin to look upon writing as a form of conflict resolution. In addition to the concrete and measurable uses of creative writing, for example, improving grammar and general written work, creative writing can enable pupils to work out their own solutions to conflicts within their own lives. This can be as simple as giving their own, real life unhappy ending a new, fictional happy ending. It can be the satisfaction of getting some form of mild 'revenge' upon a person who has caused them pain. J.K. Rowling and many other authors have admitted to using the names of awful people in their lives for evil or weak characters in their fiction.

Sometimes pupils will work out private dramas through these exercises and can be guided to do so in a healthy way. The fictionalizing of pupils' stories gives them the power to take control of their stories and change the endings, to their own satisfaction. The annoying aunt, the awful uncle, the fighting parents, the school bully, all can now get their come-uppance.

It might be worth telling your pupils that this might be their chance to work out solutions to situations where life has not seemed to be fair. Tell them that although sometimes in life there may seem to be no justice, here in their creative writing class they can get some revenge.

A good story is not made about the life of a perfect, accomplished wizard who gets everything right and easily defeats the forces of evil. The perfect story cannot be based upon the life of a princess who grows up in a lovely castle with wonderful parents, who meets a handsome prince, marries and does charity work while living in wedded bliss for the rest of her life. If pupils think about their favourite stories, characters, movies, games, they will find that their favourite characters are flawed, and perhaps could be defined as conforming in some respects to the archetypal characters described here.

It would also be boring if your favourite action hero/heroine defeated all their enemies with no trouble and was a perfect human being in every way. What would Batman do if he had killed off all the villains in the world? What would Lara Croft Tomb Raider do if there were no evil opponents left to fight – take up knitting? What would Tom do if he caught and ate Jerry, and then had an easy life?

The character profiles worked on in this exercise are extremes, and their very strong characteristics make them useful in fiction. However, pupils may realize that they also have identified a few, obviously much milder, versions of character traits discussed during this exercise, and these can be used in future story writing.

Ultimately this exercise encourages pupils to develop a form of empathy for their characters. Stories where characters are either extremely good or bad, stripped of nuances and subtleties, are simplistic and sometimes boring particularly for older and more sophisticated readers. These profiles enable pupils to develop empathy for their characters, even the bad ones. Evil characters that are complex or good characters with major human flaws to overcome before they can defeat evil will engage readers and create a compelling narrative.

8.2 The supernatural

Introduction

This exercise generates a story outline. The template that pupils are going to employ to write their outlines is used to provide structure to many, if not most, stories in which the ultimate goal is one of the many varieties of spiritual growth. More detailed information is given in the general introduction to this chapter.

Exercise 8.2:   The supernatural

Scene 1

- Introduce us to the most spiritual or religious character you wrote about using 8.1 *Character profiles*.
- Show this person in the normal course of her/his life.
- At the end of scene 1, something occurs which threatens their beliefs.

Scene 2

- Your character struggles with this obstacle in an attempt to hold on to their beliefs.
- Do they have to go somewhere to seek answers?
- At last, at the climax, they have reached a breaking point – will their belief system be restored, or destroyed?

Scene 3

- Your character takes one more desperate action to restore their life as it was.
- Is your character's belief system restored or shattered?
- Or does it survive in some modified form?

Step 1: Classroom discussion - contexts

First, to enable your pupils to deal successfully with this subject, it needs to be made very clear that religious beliefs do not have to be concerned with one of the major world religions. You can get pupils to add to a brief dictionary definition of what being devout means: 'To be devoted to a particular personal interest or cause; to be deeply and faithfully religious.'

Faith is a central theme in many of the children's favourite stories. They will be familiar with many different kinds of religious practice and spiritual belief through their own knowledge of contemporary narratives.

Examples from fiction and film

Pupils can contribute their ideas to a list of stories that they have come across where a character faces a challenge to their beliefs, such as texts studied in class.

- In *The Lion King*, Shimba must be reconciled with the ghost of his father.
- In *Brother Bear*, the man who killed the baby bear's brother must do penance for his crime.
- In *The Jungle Book*, the animals must accept that Mowgli cannot live according to the law of the jungle and must return to live with humans.
- In *Star Wars*, Luke Skywalker must undergo training to achieve a spiritual connection to his own powers before he is equipped to fight the Force.
- In the *Karate Kid*, the boy must follow a spiritual as well as a physical regime to master his sport.
- In the *Polar Express*, the children believe they are on a physical journey to the North Pole when in fact they are on a spiritual journey, to find peace within themselves.

Children will have seen situations involving characters like these in many books and films.

In earlier exercises pupils have created stories based upon a character's devotion and commitment to hobbies, people or animals.

- In 4.1 *Building atmosphere*, maybe there was a character whose life was dominated by their faith?
- In 4.2 *Sharing a room*, maybe someone wrote about a character committed to a particular sport, hobby, or movie star?

- In 4.4 *The character in the environment*, maybe pupils wrote about a character's grieving over someone's death, or their contact with the spiritual presence of someone they loved who had died?
- In 5.3 *The awkward situation*, perhaps pupils wrote about someone who was trying their best to escape from a social constraint created by religion?

It is worth noting that the character who wants to reject any formal religious or spiritual advice or development often learns, during the course of their adventures, that staying rigidly to their original belief system is not the best way to live.

If children have seen any classic quest-style films designed for older audiences they will have come across many examples of the supernatural template.

Step 2: Pair work – do you know someone like this?

Pupils can talk about characters that they consider to be the most spiritual or religious, or the character most stuck in their ways.

They should have written about such a character in 8.1 *Character profiles*. If pupils have copies of these character profiles, it might be worth sharing a selection with the whole class at this point.

- Think about why someone would want so desperately to stick to their beliefs or stick to their old routine.
- What experiences have they had that could have made them feel this way?
- Why would someone try so desperately to defeat the challenge they are faced with?

Step 3: Pair work – the challenge

Remember that you are going to describe a main character who wants to avoid, at all costs, the challenge to their world view. Work together to decide what this challenge could be. The new challenge must have something special to offer that threatens to break down your main character – the protagonist's – defences. Pupils can work out what might pose a big enough threat to their main character's belief system. They could work from the list generated earlier – Luke Skywalker (*Star Wars*), Shimba (*The Lion King*) and the Karate Kid are all very strong characters with particular qualities.

Step 4: Review of the task before pupils start writing

Having done the preliminary work, children can be reminded of the exercise. Take time to go over the following guidance with them.

Guidance

- Write a one to one and a half page outline for a story following the *Supernatural* template set out at the beginning of this section. An outline is a plan for a story, and just contains the basic plot that you want to write.
- Details such as conversations or intricate detail about the environment are not important at this stage. The object of a story outline is to give us an idea of the overall shape of the story in broad brushstrokes.
- At this stage it is possible, and much simpler, to change basic parts of the plot around to make the story work. Once the outline is written, other pupils can provide feedback as to how to make your story work better, before you have taken the trouble to write the whole story.
- Each section of the outline should just be about a paragraph long.

Start writing!

You may find it helpful to post the following questions up on the IWB in case anyone gets stuck or needs some help.

Questions to help your writing

Scene 1

- Introduce us to the most spiritual or religious person you know or have written about.
- Show this person in the normal course of her/his life.
- At the end of scene 1, something occurs which threatens their equilibrium or their belief system to the core.

Perhaps a disclosure, some traumatic event or reversal – whatever it is, it must be strong enough so the person can't ignore it.

Scene 2

- Your character struggles with this obstacle in an attempt to hold on to their belief system. It is crucial (and very challenging) to dramatize this struggle and externalize it.
- Do they have to go somewhere to seek answers? Talk to someone? Test someone? The more they seek answers, the more difficult their task becomes.
- At last, at the climax, they have reached a breaking point – will their belief system be restored, or destroyed?

Scene 3

- They take one more desperate action to restore their life as it was.
- Is your character's belief system restored or shattered?
- Or does it survive in some modified form?

Step 5: Giving feedback

Feedback should follow guidelines laid out in Chapter 4.5. As pupils read each other's work they can be reminded to ask themselves the following questions.

Feedback reminder

We should know from the outline:

- Who the main character is.
- What the main character's life was like before the challenge to their beliefs began.
- What the main character did to fight the new situation.
- Whether or not they succeeded in getting to stay the same and stick to their old beliefs.
- How the main character was affected by the events of the story: were they happy to be back where they began, or sad that they 'won' and did not change? Or perhaps delighted that they had changed?

8.3   The threat to world views

Introduction

The template that pupils are going to employ to write their outlines is used to provide structure to many, if not most, stories in which the ultimate goal is the exposure, and thus fundamental change within, the character of the liar.

Write an outline for a story following this basic pattern (each scene should be a paragraph or two long). Details such as visual elements and dialogue are not important here; the objective of a story outline is the overall story in broad brushstrokes.

Exercise 8.3:   The threat to world views

Scene 1

- Introduce us to the biggest liar you know as they go about their business.

- During this particular day, they tell a major lie.
- At the end of scene 1, it becomes suddenly apparent that the lie might be found out, threatening them with ruin.

Scene 2

- Your character takes actions to avert exposure.
- Each time they do something to maintain the deception, success is temporary, and things get worse.
- At last, matters become desperate and they plan to take one more drastic step.

Scene 3

- They take the drastic step, but their lies are exposed anyway.
- The situation blows up in a major way.
- Can you come up with a twist?

Step 1: Class discussion – examples

Pupils can contribute their ideas to a list of stories that they have come across where a character risks being uncovered as a liar. Reference can be made to texts studied in class.

Examples from fiction and film

- In *The Lion King*, Shimba's uncle is eventually uncovered as the one who killed Shimba's father.
- In *Little Red Riding Hood*, the wolf is proved not to really be grandma.
- In *Cinderella*, the step-sisters pretend to be Cinderella, but the shoe proves them to be liars.
- In *The Jungle Book*, the snake is proven to be lying when he tells Mowgli that he can trust him.

- Every time Pinocchio tells a lie, his nose grows longer.
- What happens to Mathilda?
- Or the little boy who cried 'Wolf!'?

It is worth noting that the biggest liars often learn, during the course of their adventures, that escalating their lies to avoid being caught always results in the failure of their plans.

In earlier exercises pupils may have created stories where the drama was based upon a character's decision to tell a lie, cover up the truth or get away with some deception.

- In 4.1 *Building atmosphere*, maybe there was a character that was running away from lies they had told, for example, a spy?
- In 4.2 *Sharing a room*, maybe someone wrote about a character committed to a particular pretence, for example, someone who pretended that they were really popular, or really kind, or knew lots of famous people, when that was exposed as a lie?
- In 4.4 *The character in the environment*, maybe pupils wrote about characters who pretended to be someone they were not, and thus lost a friend?
- In 5.3 *The awkward situation*, perhaps pupils wrote about someone who was trying their best to escape from a situation where all their lies would be found out?

Deception and truth are a central theme in many of the children's favourite stories. They will be familiar with many different levels of deception, and the price invariably paid for this, through their own knowledge of contemporary narratives.

Step 2: Pair work – do you know someone like this?

In pairs or small groups, pupils can talk about characters that they consider to be a candidate for the biggest liar. They should have written about such a character in 8.1 *Character profiles*. If pupils have copies of these character profiles, it might be worth sharing a selection with the whole class at this point.

Think about why someone would want so very desperately to stick to their lies? What experiences have they had that could have made them feel this way? Why would someone try so very desperately to defeat any challenges to their lies?

Step 3: Class discussion – the challenge to the liar

Remember that you are going to describe a main character who wants to avoid, at all costs, the challenge to their lies. What could this challenge be? The new challenge must have something special to offer that threatens to break down your main character – the protagonist's – defences. Pupils can work out what might pose a big enough threat to their main character's system of lying.

Step 4: Review of the task before pupils start writing

Having done the preliminary work, children can be reminded of the exercise. Take time to go over the following guidance with them.

Guidance

- Write a one to one and a half page outline for a story following *The threat to world views* template set out at the beginning of this section. An outline is a plan for a story, and just contains the basic plot that you want to write.
- Details such as conversations or intricate detail about the environment are not important at this stage. The object of a story outline is to give us an idea of the overall shape of the story in broad brushstrokes.
- At this stage it is possible, and much simpler, to change basic parts of the plot around to make the story work. Once the outline is written, other pupils can provide feedback as to how to make your story

---

work better, before you have taken the trouble to write the whole story.

- Each section of the outline should just be about a paragraph long.

Start writing!

You may find it helpful to post the following questions up on the IWB in case anyone gets stuck or needs some help.

Questions to help your writing

Scene 1

Think of the biggest liar you know – preferably someone you have strong feelings for, one way or the other. This could be the liar you wrote about for 8.1 *Character profiles*.

Introduce us to them in the normal course of their life – and again, give us a sense, as economically as possible, about their hopes, dreams, fears and how they operate. During the course of scene 1, they tell a major lie (or, at the very least, it is revealed to the readers or audience that they have told a major lie, perhaps before the story even began).

At the end of scene 1, it becomes suddenly apparent that the lie might be found out, threatening them with ruin.

Scene 2

They take actions to avert exposure (perhaps lies again), but this solves the problem only temporarily, so they must take further action.

Each time they do something to maintain the deception, their success is only temporary, and their problems only multiply.

They may have to recruit cohorts to maintain their lies, some may go along with them, but others may themselves threaten them with exposure.

At last, matters become desperate and they must take one more drastic step.

Scene 3

They take the drastic step, but their lies are exposed anyway. The situation blows up in a major way. Can you come up with a twist?

Step 5: Giving feedback

Feedback should follow guidelines laid out in Chapter 4.5. As pupils read each other's work, they can be reminded to ask themselves the following questions.

Feedback reminder

We should know from the outline:

- Who the main character is.
- What the main character's life was like before the challenge to their lies began.
- Why have they been getting away with it so far?
- What the main character did to fight the new situation.
- Whether or not they succeeded in getting to keep to their lies.
- How the main character was affected by the events of the story: were they happy to be back where they began, or sad that they 'won' and did not change? Or perhaps delighted that they had changed?

It is sometimes useful with larger classes to get groups to choose their favourite example of the exercise to share with the whole class.

8.4   Journey with destination

Introduction

Journeys, particularly the quest of a hero to achieve a goal, are a central theme in many children's favourite stories. Pupils will be familiar with many different kinds of quests, and the price invariably paid for this, through their own knowledge of contemporary narratives.

Exercise 8.4:   Journey with destination

Scene 1

- Introduce us to a character in the normal course of their life.
- They are suddenly confronted by an unavoidable need to go on a journey.
- At the end of scene 1, they know why the journey is essential, and where they are going to.

Scene 2

- They set out on their journey.
- Along the way, in succession, they come across three interesting characters in various circumstances.
- Each character makes the journey more difficult.
- After meeting the last one, it looks like your main character will not get there.

Scene 3

- Do they make it?
- Or not?
- Is there a twist you can come up with at the end?

Step 1: Class discussion

Pupils can contribute their ideas to a list of stories that they have come across where a character is forced to go upon a journey that changes their lives forever. Reference can be made to texts studied in class.

Examples from fiction and film

- In *The Wizard of Oz*, Dorothy must travel to find the Wizard or she may never get back to Kansas.
- In *The Lord of the Rings*, Frodo is quite happily living in the Shire until Gandalf shows up and asks him to go on a journey.
- In *Rat Race*, the main characters must compete in a journey across the USA.
- In the first *Shrek* film, the ugly ogre, who loves his swamp, is forced to go on a journey to rescue a princess.
- In *Shrek 2*, Donkey, Fiona and Shrek must travel to meet Fiona's parents.
- Dick Whittington must get to London.
- In *The Golden Compass*, Lyra must get to the land of the Ice Bears.
- In *Lara Croft Tomb Raider*, the woman must always leave her home to defeat the enemies.
- In *Back to the Future*, the boy must travel back in time to save his own life.
- In the *Raiders of the Lost Ark* series, the university lecturer must always travel on long quests to achieve his latest challenge.
- In *Star Wars*, Luke Skywalker must leave his home and travel across the universe to defeat the Force.

It is worth noting that the characters who are forced to set out on journeys are often very reluctant to set out, perhaps even set in their ways, and they often learn, during the course of their adventures, lessons that change the way they behave, once they finally make it back home.

In earlier exercises pupils may have created stories where the drama was based upon a character's decision to set out on a journey.

- In 4.2 *Sharing a room*, maybe someone wrote about a character committed to staying put, who was forced to leave on a journey?
- In 4.4 *The character in the environment*, maybe pupils wrote about a character who left on a long journey and returned later, a very changed person?
- In 7.1 *Revolt, revenge, escape*, perhaps pupils wrote about someone who was trying their best to travel far away from some situation they were trapped in?

Step 2: Pair work – who is your character?

Pupils can work in pairs to create some ideas for the kinds of character they would like to send on a journey. They need to come up with some thoughts as to the problems that their character might run into along the way, and how their main character might be changed by going on this journey.

Step 3: Review of the task before pupils start writing

Having done the preliminary work, children can be reminded of the exercise. Take time to go over the following guidance with them.

Guidance

- Write a one to one and a half page outline for the journey templates you have worked on in this book. An outline is a plan for a story, and just contains the basic plot that you want to write.
- Details such as conversations or intricate detail about the environment are not important at this stage. The object of a story outline is

to give us an idea of the overall shape of the story in broad brush-strokes.

- At this stage it is possible, and much simpler, to change basic parts of the plot around to make the story work. Once the outline is written, other pupils can provide feedback as to how to make your story work better, before you have taken the trouble to write the whole story.
- Each section of the outline should just be about a paragraph long.

Start writing!

You may find it helpful to post the following questions up on the IWB in case anyone gets stuck or needs some help.

Questions to help your writing

Scene 1

- Introduce us to a character in the normal course of their life (consider using any of the characters you have written about, perhaps from 8.1 *Character profiles*), someone who would be particularly tested by the story.
- Use whatever clever and visual means you have to establish quickly who they are and the patterns of their life. For example, in the first few minutes of the *Shrek* film, we get to see Shrek and all his horrible habits, and the big KEEP OUT sign that he nails to his swamp, and how happy he is, all alone, in his swamp.
- In scene 1, they are suddenly confronted by the need to go on a journey. The necessity must be strong. There is no way out of it. Perhaps they have to convey a message, or get something. The journey can be anything from a trip across the room to one across the galaxy.

- At the end of scene 1, they (and the readers, or audience) know what the necessity is, and the destination.

Scene 2

- They set out on their journey.
- Along the way, in succession, they meet three interesting characters in various different circumstances.
- Each character makes the journey more difficult.
- After the last encounter, it seems they will not make it to their destination at all.

Scene 3

- Resolution: do they make it or not?
- Is there a twist you can come up with at the end? For example, the princess is an ogre as well, or the Wizard of Oz is just a fake, or at the last moment, the hero cannot find the strength to throw the ring into the volcano? Is the place different from the way they (or the audience) originally conceived it?

Step 4: Giving feedback

Feedback should follow guidelines laid out in Chapter 4.5. As pupils read each other's work they can be reminded to ask themselves the following questions.

Feedback reminder

We should know from the outline the answers to the following:

- Whose story is it?
- What does your main character, the protagonist want?
- What is at stake?

- What is the main tension?
- What do the readers hope or fear will happen?
- What is the character's life dream?
- How does the character change during the story?
- What is your theme?

If pupils are unfamiliar with these questions, it would be worth referring again to 7.3 *Story questions*.

8.5   The escape

Introduction

This exercise is called *The escape* because children are going to be encouraged to escape from their own world and point of view. It is the last exercise in the book, and should produce the best work.

This exercise is significantly different from all the other exercises, because it almost serves as all the other exercises put together. A child might be writing about a royal wedding, using the *Character least capable of love* template from 8.1 *Character profiles*, or about an Afghani orphan escaping to become a billionaire, using 7.1 *Revolt, revenge, escape*. Every story ever told and every template ever described in this book is up for grabs. The best guidance we could give to teachers would be for their school to buy every pupil a copy of this book!

Through using non-fiction news or magazine stories as the inspiration for fiction, children can finally digest the fact that in fiction, writers gain the power to change and transform material that is upsetting or uncomfortable, which can give children a position of power and allow them to develop a different outcome.

Above all it encourages them to see that these templates and tools are transferable and can be used to create a vast range of stories, plays and even poems.

Exercise 8.5:   The escape

Children are given a photograph or a story taken from the previous weekend's newspapers and magazines. You will have to prepare for this: see box below.

- The pupils will be asked to study the photo or read the story that they have been given.
- Then they have to write a story based upon some element of the photo or story they have been given, from the point of view of a character in the story.

Exercises used in earlier chapters, from 4.3 *Getting ready for a date* to 8.1 *Character profiles* (e.g. 'Most ambitious person') or 7.1 *Revolt, revenge, escape,* can be used as templates to shape their stories.

Pupils can also have the option of writing in another format, for example, creating a poem, or a short scene from a play, as well as a story, but whatever kind of writing they choose to produce it should still be based upon the story or photo that they have been given, and if possible follow one of the templates provided in earlier exercises.

Step 1: Preparation work

To prepare for this you will need a collection of weekend newspapers and magazines. These should include tabloid newspapers and broadsheets that contain a good range of international news stories. Go through the newspapers and magazines and cut out any stories that you think could be used by children to complete this exercise. Use your own judgement in the selection of age-appropriate material.

It can be a useful exercise to give pupils who have until now been very limited in writing stories that the teacher judges will best stretch their imaginations, for example:

- A girl who only wants to write about princesses and princes could be given the story of some miners trapped underground for many days or weeks.

- A boy who only wants to write about his sporting heroes or about computer games can be given a story about a child in South Africa who has to look after four younger brothers and sisters, and find food for them every day.
- A pupil who is obsessed by celebrities can be asked to write a poem from the point of view of a famous person having a horrible life as a result of their celebrity.

Using this exercise pupils have been encouraged to come up with some interesting and excellent storylines as described below.

Examples from non-fiction, news and magazine features

One pupil was given a story from the *International Guardian* about a young girl of 9 who had to support her whole family in East Timor because she had lost her mother and father. The pupil chose to take material from the story and give it a happy ending, by shaping the story using the 'Most ambitious person' template from 8.1 *Character profiles*.

Another pupil was given a tabloid newspaper story about the exploits of the model, Kate Moss. The child chose to write a story based upon the template 4.3 *Getting ready for a date*, so that we could see an imaginary Kate getting ready to go out, and then returning from her disastrous night out, using information taken from the newspaper article, but written sympathetically and from Kate's point of view.

A story in *Saga Magazine* about people who had changed their lives around in mid-life described a man whose wife had committed suicide because she could not conceive a child. He gave up his lucrative job, moved to Nepal and set up an orphanage for abandoned Nepalese girls; he has adopted a Nepalese daughter of his own. The orphanage is named after his wife. One pupil took the same article and developed a story based upon the template 'Most ambitious person' from 8.1 *Character profiles*.

Pupils should be given a choice of at least two photos or stories to choose from, that they could use as inspiration for this exercise, possibly working out in pairs which stories they would like to work with.

Step 2: Pair work – review of past exercises

Pupils can work in pairs to create a list of their favourites from the exercises in Chapters 4 and 5 in this book. This might be, for example, 4.2 *Sharing a room*, 4.3 *Getting ready for a date*, 5.3 *The awkward situation* or 7.1 *Revolt, revenge, escape*. Pupils discuss the articles that they have been given, then try to come up with ways that the stories they are reading might be shaped to fit one of the earlier story templates.

Step 3: Review of the task before pupils start writing

Having done the preliminary work, children can be reminded of the exercise. Take time to go over the following guidance with them.

Guidance

- Write a one to one and a half page outline for a story following any of the exercises or the templates set out at the beginning of this section. An outline is a plan for a story, and just contains the basic plot that you want to write.
- Details such as conversations or intricate detail about the environment are not important at this stage. The object of a story outline is to give us an idea of the overall shape of the story in broad brushstrokes.
- At this stage it is possible, and much simpler, to change basic parts of the plot around to make the story work. Once the outline is written, other pupils can provide feedback as to how to make your story work better, before you have taken the trouble to write the whole story.
- Each section of the outline should just be about a paragraph long.

Start writing!

At this point children have selected their own story or been given one from a newspaper, and they have been asked to apply the exercise or template of their choice to the story from the newspaper. Pupils should be reminded that they are now working independently. If they cannot remember the exercise clearly, it may help if they ask the teacher for a copy of the book.

Step 4: Giving feedback

Feedback should follow guidelines laid out in Chapter 4.5. As pupils read each other's work they can be reminded to ask themselves the following questions.

> **Feedback reminder**
>
> We should know from the outline the answers to the following:
>
> * Whose story is it?
> * What does your main character, the protagonist, want?
> * What is at stake?
> * What is the main tension?
> * What do the readers hope or fear will happen?
> * What is the character's life dream?
> * How does the character change during the story?
> * What is your theme?

If pupils are unfamiliar with these questions, it would be worth referring again to 7.3 *Story questions*.

Summary

We have found this exercise to be among the most transformative of all. It enables pupils to write outside their own life experiences and to think beyond the limits of their own lives, towns, regions and country.

They are encouraged to write, sympathetically, from the point of view of a character that they might not even like and to discover that wonderful stories can be found in the world around us. They will understand that the world around them is rich with incredible stories waiting to be told and that writers can, and do, use everything that they come across to feed their creative well. They should by now realize that the exercises that they have completed can be transferred and used as a foundation for a multitude of narratives.

The work produced from this exercise will be incredible; you may be amazed by the stretch and span of the children's imaginations and capacity for empathy. Children can also learn that in fiction we can control endings; we can change and transform material that is upsetting or uncomfortable, such as news coverage of events showing victims of disasters, which can give children a position of power and allow them to develop a different outcome. In fact, through inspirational work, people worldwide are working to change multiple unhappy endings.

Above all it encourages children to see that these templates and tools are transferable and can be used to create a vast range of stories, plays and even poems.

Conclusion

CHAPTER 9

'I write, therefore I am': towards a theory of writing pedagogy

Introduction

'Cogito ergo sum' (I think, therefore I am) was written by the philosopher Descartes in *Discourse on the Method* in 1637; it is often used as 'I write, therefore I am' and it is with this variation that we would like to begin the final chapter in this book.

During the writing of this book we have worked towards providing teachers with a blueprint for teaching writing that goes beyond meeting curriculum outcomes and statements. However, this is challenging because this philosophy is so deeply entrenched in teacher professional action, teacher education and teacher professional development. We have seen in Chapter 1 that there is a body of research and theorizing into the teaching of writing which can contribute to teacher practice in the field. Chapter 2 engages in the field of creativity and argues for the classroom as a creative space and encourages teachers to use talk and dialogue to emulate the context of a creative industry. Chapter 3 supplies an overview of the National Curriculum (DfEE 1999), the Literacy Strategy and the Primary National Strategy (Department for Education and Skills (DfES) 2006) and begins to raise wider questions about the value assigned to writing within statutory testing, and explores the idea that 'good writing' might be something that is not so easily identifiable.

In attempting to frame broad notions of writing pedagogy by looking at teaching writing in schools over the past hundred years, we have established that there is no one-shot solution to the endeavour of teaching writing – teaching writing is as difficult as writing is. We all find writing challenging and this is further exacerbated by the fact that it can be a very high risk activity because it long ago became a 'gatekeeping' activity. In many cases writing is used to assess ability to compose a one-shot piece, which is often the sole judgement of the writer's ability.

Professional writers find writing difficult too. John Banville, an Irish author who wrote *The Book of Evidence* (1989), which was shortlisted for the Man Booker Prize, writes in a powerful way about the difficulty of writing:

> Civilisation's greatest single invention is the sentence. In it, we can say anything. That saying, however, is difficult and peculiarly painful. . . . The struggle of writing is fraught with a specialised form of anguish, the anguish of knowing one will never get it right, that one will always fail, and that all one can hope to do is 'fail better', as Beckett recommends. The pleasure of writing is in the preparation, not the execution, and certainly not in the thing executed.
>
> (John Banville, quoted in Flood 2009)

This is an insight into the world of the professional writer, but also a strong admission that writing, even for those who do it as a vocation, is difficult. Even authors such as John Banville or Colm Tóibín quote Samuel Johnson's 300-year-old statement that 'no man but a blockhead ever wrote, except for money'. It is important that we keep in our sights that writing for those most accomplished in it and awarded for it, remains evasive, but that the pleasures can be found in the preparation for writing – which is perhaps a lot of what is provided in this book for readers and users.

Writing as transformation

It is often suggested that learning is about transformation (Healy 2008; Kalantzis and Cope 2005; Walshe 2010) and that transformation can provide a basis for improved learner engagement and performance. There is no doubt that writing can be transformative and the exercises in this book aim to provide a contextual framework for this type of learning. The exercises in this book encourage writers to engage in thinking and to create texts which contain evidence of the transformation of their ideas, and their thoughts and hence improve their learning.

Everett (2005) writes at length about the value gained by the learner through writing creatively; his discussion is wide ranging and focuses most closely on creative writing courses at university level. According to Everett (2005) the teaching of creative writing is transformative because it delivers analytical skills, social skills, the skills of giving and receiving feedback, and truly communicative skills in a purposeful focused way. Writing frees us and gives us wings, and by engaging in teaching creative writing we can extend learners and justify teaching which enables learners to understand more about themselves.

Some of life's challenges can be explored from the safety of the exercises in this book and learners can engage in some higher order thinking and problem solving through plot construction and character design. Importantly, at all times, teachers must reinforce and restate the fact that in these exercises pupils are dealing with fiction, creating stories. Below are some of the themes that emerge from the earlier exercises in this book.

Loss

A crucial theme in narrative composition is loss. In every story, at some point, the main character will suffer some sort of loss or setback. During the exercises in this book children have had the opportunity to experiment with, perhaps master and certainly become familiar with one of the most fundamental components of good storytelling.

Family life

Another exercise in this book has offered a chance to discuss family dynamics, how the children's own personalities interact with those of others, methods of conflict resolution, and a form of acceptance of variety of human personality both within our lives and our schools. They are beginning to get an understanding of the idea that the minute detail and irritations of daily life can be exploited to add detail to great stories.

Sometimes pupils will work out their own dramas through these exercises. The fictionalizing of their stories enables pupils to take control of their stories and change things around, in whatever way they wish.

Conflict resolution

In addition to the concrete and measurable uses of creative writing, for example, improving grammar and general written work, creative writing can enable pupils to work out their own solutions to conflicts within their own lives. This can be as simple as resolving their own problems with a new happy ending or of getting their own back on someone who has caused them pain, perhaps by using the person's name for evil or weak characters in their stories.

Bullying

A further exercise in this book, particularly the group discussion and sharing of ideas about the 'Most repressed or enslaved person', can be used to reinforce any work teachers are already doing to combat bullying in their schools. A pupil known to be a bully could be forced to work out why someone might become a victim. This exercise should encourage the building of empathy and understanding, because we cannot understand a character unless we have a clear idea of their motivation.

The exercises in this book work by stretching and reinforcing pupils' development of the newly emerging and eventually sophisticated range of social skills that they will need to operate successfully in a range of environments. They may also be aware that skills of persuasion are actually a vital survival tool both in the pecking order of their own school playgrounds and in the world of work and outside endeavour that their parents occupy.

The children will have a chance to change the ending of the story for their characters later on (when the victim has a chance to 'revolt, get revenge, or escape') and pupils will be able to take control of their character's fate. Sometimes getting the bully to work out how the victim could revolt against oppression, or getting the pupil who is a victim to write about how an ambitious child achieves their goals, could provide a practical way of working out a problem.

Teachers must reinforce and re-state the fact that pupils in this class are dealing with fiction, creating stories, but using the fabric of their own lives and experiences as a basis for their writing. It is worth repeating that creative writing is not a form of therapy and these exercises should never be used with this goal. However, fictionalizing life events does provide children with a safe place in which to share events that have had a strong emotional impact upon them. It can be said, 'In life there may be no justice, but here in creative writing we can get our revenge.'

A creative writing pedagogy: 'in relationship'

Sawyer (2004: 17): notes: 'Teaching has always involved the creative appropriation of curricula within the situated practice of a given classroom.' Thus if teaching is a creative profession, teachers could be deemed to work in a creative industry. The exercises in this book enable us to think more about teaching and the ways that learning is mediated in our classrooms – in particular how we can bring learners to engage in the development of new ideas and thus creative writing.

The central idea of many of the exercises and much of the coverage in the early chapters of this book has focused on the development of relationships (between both the teacher and pupils and between pupils) within the creative writing classroom. Craft (1997, 2005) refers to her own research where she talks about 'creativity' emerging through dialogue as a notion of 'being in relationship'. She sees this relationship as having four facets which may or may not work together or individually.

Craft's (1997) 'being in relationship' directly depicts 'creativity' as emerging through dialogue. Stables (2003) gives us a clear framework with which to think about classroom dialogue:

- Context 1: teacher–student and teacher–class dialogue
- Context 2: between student dialogue
- Context 3: within student dialogue – student and text
- Context 4: within student dialogue – reflection and problem solving

If we look at the work of Stables (2003) and his research into classroom dialogue, this allows us a systematic way of thinking about the opportunities for 'being in relationship' in the context of classroom talk. Clearly the exercises in this book provide opportunities for dialogue of each of the kinds above. Perhaps further detail will focus the discussion a little more.

Context 1: teacher–student and teacher–class dialogue

Much of this type of dialogue is characterized by the traditional teacher-led initiation–response–evaluation (IRE). Stables (2003) calls this asymmetrical because the power is held by the teacher and none is invested with the learner. This involves the teacher asking a question and one or more students answering, followed by the teacher providing an evaluation of the students' answer. The existence, dominance and monopoly of IRE in classrooms across time and geography is in no doubt, and teachers use this in a balanced and skilful way a lot of the time.

Context 2: between student dialogue

Often in response to the recognition of the dominance of IRE teachers have increased collaborative talk in their primary classrooms. A focus on the centrality of talk in the primary classroom and developing a classroom culture of dialogue, will result in a more symmetrical notion of classroom interaction where power is distributed more evenly. What is seen to be an important element of this symmetrical notion of classroom interaction, is that the negotiation of the task can at times be more important for learning than the successful completion of the task.

Context 3: within student dialogue – student and text

In the 1920s Vygotsky (1986) conceived the idea of the learner's 'inner speech', which suggests that the learner often has to engage with a 'text' or some type of language based activity which is physically separate from the teacher. However, this 'inner speech' is something that teachers do not often think about or pay attention to.

We know very little about the quality of this speech or dialogue – perhaps if the pupils are quiet while they are reading the book, or focused while listening to the teacher read, and we judge the 'atmosphere' as being focused or settled, then this 'within student' dialogue will be working well.

Context 4: within student dialogue – reflection and problem solving

This aspect of the 'within student' dialogue is less clear to teachers and those who write and disseminate curriculum. However, the creative writing exercises in this book provide enabling contexts where problem solving and reflection, rather than content are at the centre of the curriculum.

Writing by design

So what then is 'writing by design' and what role for the teacher in this community of engagement? Research in the Slovak Republic (Gmitrova and Gmitrova 2003: 242) found that children's creativity was far greater when teacher interaction was not 'frontal directed' and was instead 'gently facilitating'. The exercises in this book provide a perfect vehicle for teachers to give some clear instructions, but most of the time the teacher is facilitating and having the writers engage in the kind of classroom dialogue that allows creativity to emerge. Most importantly these exercises create opportunities not only within student dialogue – student and text, but also within student dialogue – reflection and problem solving, and it is this type of student dialogue which engages the creativity and moves writers to produce new and exciting final products.

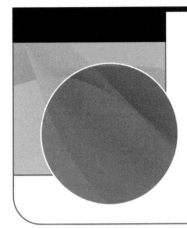

References

Alexander, R.J. (2001) *Culture and Pedagogy: International Comparisons in Primary Education.* Oxford: Blackwell.

Alexander, R.J. (2004) *Towards Dialogic Teaching: Rethinking Classroom Talk*, 2nd edn. Cambridge: Dialogos.

Alexander, R.J. (2008) *Towards Dialogic Teaching: Rethinking Classroom Talk*, 4th edn. York: Dialogos.

Andrews, R. (2009) English at school in England. In Maybin, J. and Swann, J. (eds) *The Routledge Companion to English Language Studies.* London: Routledge.

Arts and Business, MMC Arts, Business and Employees Award (2004) *Bravo!* Available at www.businessinarts-nw.org.uk/2804.000_Bravo_Brochure_v5.pdf (accessed 31 March 2011).

Bakhtin, M. (1981) *The Dialogic Imagination.* Austin, TX: University of Texas Press.

Barnes, D. (1976) *From Communication to Curriculum.* Harmondsworth: Penguin.

Bernstein, B. (1975) *Class, Codes and Control, Volume 3: Towards a Theory of Educational Transmission.* London: Routledge & Kegan Paul.

Britton, J. (1970) *Language and Learning.* London: Penguin.

Britton, J. (1972) The present state of theory and knowledge relating to English teaching. *English in Australia* 22: 9–12.

Bruner, J. (1978) The role of dialogue in language acquisition. In Sinclair, A., Jarvella, R., and Levelt, W. (eds) *The Child's Conception of Language.* New York: Springer.

Callaghan, M., Knapp, P., and Noble, M. (1993) *Text and Context: Using Functional Grammar in the Classroom.* Erskineville, NSW: Metropolitan East Disadvantaged Schools Program.

Christie, F., Devlin, B., Freebody, P., Luke, A., Martin, J.R., Threadgold, T., and Walton, C. (1991) *Teaching English Literacy: A Project of National Significance on the Pre-service Preparation of Teachers for Teaching English Literacy*, Volume 2. Canberra, ACT: Department for Employment, Education and Training.

Cope, B. and Kalantzis, M. (1993) *The Powers of Literacy.* London: Falmer.

ᴌetting the Buggers be Creative. London: Continuum.

, Knowledge about Language: System and Pedagogy. Unpublished PhD ᴊames Cook University, Australia.

ᴧ. (1997) Identity and creativity: Education for post-modernism? *Teacher Development: A International Journal for Teachers' Professional Development* 1(1): 83–96.

Craft, A. (2005) *Creativity in Schools: Tensions and Dilemmas*. London: Routledge.

Cremin, T., Mottram, M., Collins, F., Powell, S., and Safford, K. (2009) Teachers as readers: Building communities of readers. *Literacy* 43(1): 11–19.

Department for Children, Schools and Families (DCSF) (2008) *Talk for Writing*. London: DCSF.

Department for Children, Schools and Families (DCSF) (2009) *Independent Review of the Primary Curriculum: Final Report* (Rose Review). London: HMSO.

Department for Culture, Media and Sport (DCMS) (2006) *Government Response to Paul Roberts' Report on Nurturing Creativity in Young People*. Available at www.musicmanifesto.co.uk/assets/x/50364 (accessed 31 March 2011).

Department for Education and Employment (DfEE) (1999) *The National Curriculum for England: English*. London: DfEE.

Department for Education and Skills (DfES) (2006) *Primary National Strategy. Primary Framework for Literacy and Mathematics*. London: DfES.

Department of Education and Science (DES) (1975) *A Language for Life: Report of the Committee of Inquiry Appointed by the Secretary of State for Education and Science* (Bullock Report). London: HMSO.

Derewianks, B. (1991) *Exploring How Texts Work*. Sydney: Primary English Teaching Association.

Dixon, J.L. (1975) *Growth through English: Set in the Perspective of the Seventies*. London: Oxford University Press for the National Association for the Teaching of English.

Everett, N. (2005) Creative writing and English. *Cambridge Quarterly* 34(3): 231–242.

Flood, A. (2009) Writing for a living: A joy or a chore? *Guardian*, 3 March. Available at www.guardian.co.uk/books/2009/mar/03/authors-on-writing (accessed 26 April 2011).

Flower, L. and Hayes, J.R. (1977) Problem solving strategies and the writing process. *College English* 39: 21–32.

Gmitrova, V. and Gmitrova, J. (2003) The impact of teacher-directed and child-directed pretend play on cognitive competence in kindergarten children. *Early Childhood Education Journal* 30(4): 240–252.

Goodman, K. (1986) *What's Whole in Whole Language*. Ontario, Canada: Ashtons Scholastic.

Graff, H.J. (1987) *The Labyrinths of Literacy: Reflections on Literacy Past and Present*. London: Falmer.

Graves, D. (1983) *Writing: Teachers and Children at Work*. Portsmouth, NH: Heinemann.

Halliday, M.A.K. (1975) *Learning How to Mean: Explorations in the Development of Language*. London: Edward Arnold.

Halliday, M.A.K. (1985) *An Introduction to Functional Grammar*. London: Edward Arnold.

Healy, A.H. (2008) Expanding student capacities: Learning by design pedagogy. In Healy, A.H. (ed.) *Multiliteracies and Diversity in Education: New Pedagogies for Expanding Landscapes*. Oxford: Oxford University Press.

Hilton, M. (2001) Writing process and progress: Where do we go from here? *English Education* 35(1): 4–11.

Holland, S. (2003) *Creative Writing: A Good Practice Guide*. London: Royal Holloway College, University of London. Available at www.english. heacademy.ac.uk/archive/publications/reports/cwguide.pdf (accessed 11 April 2011).

Kalantzis, M. and Cope, B. (2005) *Learning by Design*. Available at http:// newlearningonline.com/kalantzisandcope/ (accessed 31 March 2011).

Loveless, A. (2005) Thinking about creativity: Developing ideas, making things happen. In Wilson, A. (ed.) *Creativity in Primary Education*. Exeter: Learning Matters.

MacLusky, J. (2009) Creative writing: Can it be taught? Paper presented at IHCA Seminar Series, University of Worcester, February.

Martin, J. and Rothery, J. (1980) *Working Papers in Linguistics*. Sydney: Linguistics Department, University of Sydney.

Mercer, N. (1995) *The Guided Construction of Knowledge*. Bristol: Multilingual Matters.

Mercer, N. and Dawes, L. (2008) The value of exploratory talk. In Mercer, N. and Hodgkinson, S. (eds) *Exploring Talk in School*. London: Sage.

Mercer, N., Wegerif, R., and Dawes, L. (1999) Children's talk and the development of reasoning in the classroom. *British Journal of Educational Research* 25(1): 95–111.

Nolan, V. (2004) Creativity: The antidote to the argument culture. In Fryer, M. (ed.) *Creativity and Cultural Diversity*. Leeds: The Creativity Centre Educational Trust.

Office for Standards in Education, Children's Services and Skills (Ofsted) (2009) *English at the Crossroads: An Evaluation of English in Primary and Secondary Schools 2005/08*. London: HMSO.

Peha, S. (2002) *What is Good Writing?* Available at www.ttms.org/PDFs/13 What is Good Writing v001 (Full).pdf (accessed 31 March 2011).

Sawyer, R.K. (2004) Creative teaching: Collaborative discussion as disciplined improvisation. *Educational Researcher* 33(1): 12–20.

Sinclair, J. and Coulthard, M. (1992) Toward an analysis of discourse. In Coulthard, M. (ed.) *Advances in Spoken Discourse Analysis*. London: Routledge.

Stables, A. (2003) Learning, identity and classroom dialogue. *Journal of Educational Enquiry* 4(1): 1–18.

Sternberg, R.J. and Lubart, T. (1995) *Defying the Crowd: Cultivating Creativity in a Culture of Conformity*. New York: Free Press.

̠) *The Blazing Drive: Creative Potential.* Buffalo, NY: Bearly.

̠962) *Thought and Language.* Cambridge, MA: MIT Press.

̠s. (1978) *Mind in Society: The Development of Higher Mental Processes.* ̠ridge, MA: Harvard University Press.

̠sky, L.S. (1986) *Thought and Language*, revised edn. Cambridge, MA: MIT Press.

Wallas, G. (1926) *The Art of Thought.* New York: Harcourt Brace.

Walshe, M. (2010) *Multimodal Literacy: Researching Classroom Practice.* Sydney: Primary English Teaching Association.

Walshe, R.D. (1981) *Donald Graves in Australia: Children Want to Write.* Sydney NSW: Primary English Teaching Association.

Wandor, M. (2003) Appendix B: A Creative Writing Manifesto. In Holland, S., *Creative Writing: A Good Practice Guide.* London: Royal Holloway College, University of London. Available at www.english.heacademy.ac.uk/archive/publications/reports/cwguide.pdf (accessed 11 April 2011).

Wells, G. (1999) *Dialogic Inquiry: Towards a Socio-cultural Practice and Theory of Education (Learning in Doing: Social, Cognitive and Computational Perspectives).* Cambridge: Cambridge University Press.

Whitehead, F. (1966) *The Disappearing Dais: A Study of the Principles and Practice of English Teaching.* London: Chatto & Windus.

Wolfe, S. and Alexander, R. (2008) *Argumentation and Dialogic Thinking: Alternative Pedagogies for a Changing World.* Available at www.beyondcurrenthorizons.org.uk (accessed 14 February 2010).

Wragg, E.C. (2005) *The Art and Science of Teaching and Learning: The Selected Works of Ted Wragg.* London: Routledge.

Index

DEVELOPING LITERACY AND CREATIVE WRITING THROUGH STORYMAKING
Story Strands for 7-12 Year Olds

Steve Bowkett

978-0-335-24158-3
Paperback / 2010

Supported by a companion website that includes downloadable images from the book, additional activities and games.

www.openup.co.uk/storymaking-bowkett

This exciting practical resource is full of immediately usable activities to help children develop their literacy skills and creative writing abilities.

The activities are creative and intellectual, and can be used to highlight different aspects of the writing process such as:

- Exploring the varied meanings of certain words through association webs
- Moving from simple to more complex sentences
- Learning how to enrich writing using vivid adjectives, verbs and adverbs
- Understanding how to use connectives more insightfully
- Creating narrative refinements such as subplots, flashbacks and 'cliffhangers' out of basic plot sequences

A 'thinking skills' agenda underpins each story strand game, and many promote speaking and listening skills by encouraging discussion and collaborative exploration of the images.

MOVING ONTO KEY STAGE 1
Improving Transition from the Early Years
Foundation Stage

Julie Fisher

9780335238460 (Paperback)
2010

eBook also available

The author considers recent evidence about how children learn and questions
whether current practice in Key Stage 1 optimises these ways of learning.
Challenging the reliance on teacher-directed activity, she asks whether
introducing more child-initiated learning could offer children a more appropriate
balance of learning opportunities.

Key issues include:

- The place of play in Key Stage 1
- Organizing the learning day to include child-initiated activity
- Observation and assessment
- Planning
- The role of the teacher

www.openup.co.uk

CRITICAL THINKING ACROSS THE CURRICULUM

Developing Critical Thinking Skills, Literacy and Philosophy in the Primary Classroom

Mal Leicester and Denise Taylor

9780335238798 (Paperback)
2010

Learning how to be critical and think for one's self are key development steps in the education process. Developing critical thinking is vital for supporting children to become independent learners.

This fun, practical book is very easy to use in the classroom and is designed to help children:

- Understand key critical thinking concepts.
- Develop critical thinking skills.
- Understand different types of reasoning and knowledge in all areas of the curriculum.
- Draw on their natural wonder and curiosity to engage in philosophical discussion.
- Develop reasoning skills in relation to moral dilemmas and the choices of every day life.

www.openup.co.uk

OPEN UNIVERSITY PRESS
McGraw - Hill Education